Retroactive Legislation

Retroactive Legislation

Daniel E. Troy

The AEI Press

Publisher for the American Enterprise Institute
WASHINGTON, D.C.

1998

Publication of this volume was made possible by a generous grant from the Rollin M. Gerstacker Foundation to the American Enterprise Institute in support of AEI's program of studies in government regulation and legal policy.

Distributed to the Trade by National Book Network, 15200 NBN Way, Blue Ridge Summit, PA 17214. To order call toll free 1-800-462-6420 or 1-717-794-3800. For all other inquiries please contact the AEI Press, 1150 Seventeenth Street, N.W., Washington, D.C. 20036 or call 1-800-862-5801.

Library of Congress Cataloging-in-Publication Data
    Retroactive legislation / Dan Troy.
      p.   cm.
    Includes bibliographical references and index.
    ISBN 0-8447-4022-5 (cloth) ISBN 978-0-8447-4023-2

    1. Retroactive laws—United States.   I. Title.
    KF420.T76   1998
    340'.115'0973—dc21   97-52784
                                                     CIP

THE AEI PRESS
Publisher for the American Enterprise Institute
1150 17th Street, N.W., Washington, D.C. 20036

*To Judge Robert H. Bork, whose commitment
to the rule of law I hope this volume reflects*

CONTENTS

PART TWO
CONSTITUTIONAL CONSTRAINTS ON RETROACTIVE CIVIL LEGISLATION

4 THE EX POST FACTO CLAUSES 47

5 THE BILL OF ATTAINDER CLAUSES 56

6 THE CONTRACTS CLAUSE 60

7 THE FIFTH AMENDMENT'S PROHIBITION AGAINST UNCOMPENSATED TAKINGS 66

ACKNOWLEDGMENTS

This volume was commissioned by the American Enterprise Institute and was inspired by Christopher DeMuth, whose insightful comments proved invaluable. I am grateful for the comments of Thomas W. Brunner, Ernest Gellhorn, John C. Harrison, John F. Manning, John O. McGinnis, J. Gregory Sidak, Bill Siegel, my brothers Gil and Tevi Troy, as well as all those who shared their thoughts at the AEI symposium on this topic. The standard disclaimers apply. I am also thankful for the assistance of Allison R. Hayward, Miranda Perry, and Kaija Clark, as well as the yeoman efforts of my editor, Cheryl Weissman. I could not have written this piece without the incalculable support of my wife, Dr. Cheryl Horowitz Troy, and the sacrifices of my children, Aaron Lev and Leora Jordana. I also wish to thank my colleagues and partners at Wiley, Rein & Fielding for their indulgence, cooperation, and support. The views expressed herein are mine alone, and do not reflect the views of Wiley, Rein & Fielding or its clients.

1

❖

INTRODUCTION

A retroactive law is truly a monstrosity. Law has to do with the governance of human conduct by rules. To speak of governing today by rules that will be enacted tomorrow is to talk in blank prose.

LON FULLER, *The Morality of Law* [1]

As Lon Fuller accurately states, Anglo-American tradition is profoundly hostile to "retroactive" laws. This hostility is embodied in our Constitution, most notably in the prohibitions on ex post facto laws. Not changing the rules after the game has been played is considered an element of fundamental fairness. Books on child training, on how to improve marriages, and on effective management all emphasize the importance of establishing a rule, sticking with it, and providing notice before changing it.

A passage in H. Clay Trumbull's 1890 *Hints on Child Training* exemplifies this sentiment. He writes that "as a rule, a child ought not to be punished except for an offense that, at the time of its committal, was known by the child to be an offense deserving of punishment. It is no more fair for a parent to impose a penalty to an offense after the offense is committed, than it is for a civil government to pass an ex post facto law, by which punishment is to be awarded for offenses committed before the law was passed."[2]

The problem, though, is that in one sense almost all legislation can be characterized as "retroactive," if by that notion we mean a law that may surprise people who have made decisions in reliance on the existing legal regime. The technical reason for this verity is that the operation of almost all legislation depends on antecedent facts. As a result, legislation inevitably has the potential to upset settled, investment-backed expectations.

To take a basic example, a real estate tax increase that operates prospectively raises the taxes on a house that a taxpayer bought in the past, perhaps in the expectation that he or she was buying in a low-tax jurisdiction. The moment the legislature raises the tax on the house it is worth less, because the market takes account of the value of the regulatory change as soon as it becomes publicly known. To take just one more example, consider a prospective repeal of the tax exemption for interest on an outstanding municipal bond.[3] Without referring to the past or changing the past legal consequences of any past event, the law has substantially affected the existing interest of the homeowner or taxpayer. Professor Jill Fisch puts it simply: prospective laws "in fact affect prior transactions."[4]

Similarly, as Professors Douglas Kmiec and John McGinnis have noted, "Almost all laws operate retrospectively in that they must defeat the subjective expectations of those who planned their conduct according to the existing law."[5] Indeed, the twentieth-century legal scholar Fuller says that "if every time a man relied on existing law in arranging his affairs, he were made secure against any change in legal rules, the whole body of our law would be ossified forever."[6] Even the most conservative among us concede the importance of accommodating some legal change. Professor David Slawson is thus correct in concluding that "reliance on existing rules . . . must be sacrificed to some extent to the need for change."[7]

New laws must always be read in light of existing laws. When a new law impinges on interests created under an old law, which law should be followed? All the interests created under the old law cannot be respected, or legal change would be impossible. But fundamental fairness requires that reasonable expectations be preserved and notice be given of the effect of new laws. Fairness may also require compensation to parties whose expectations are thwarted.

For centuries, courts, legislators, and commentators have wrestled with the problem of precisely how to designate the point at which a law is sufficiently harmful to existing interests so that it merits being classified as "retroactive." Defining a law as retroactive has rarely ended the analysis, however. The debate then becomes whether such laws, or which subcategory of retroactive laws, should be prohibited.

The ultimate question in dealing with the problem of retroactive legislation is, therefore, to define when a law is sufficiently different from other laws, despite their (almost inevitable) retrospective effects, to merit the label "retroactive." Secondarily, we must identify which of those are *illegitimately* retroactive laws. There are two closely related parts to this inquiry. The first is definitional: when is a law retroactive? The second is normative: is the retroactive law justified? The answer to the second question turns on yet another normative inquiry—namely, in Slawson's terms, to what extent is one willing "to sacrifice reliance on existing rules" to accommodate "the need for change?"

This monograph seeks to address that vexing question by, first, seeking to distinguish among forms of laws. Next, in an effort to answer the second question—which (retrospective) laws are illegitimately retroactive—this study examines the arguments against retroactive legislation. The inquiry suggests that there may be some few laws that are retroactive in form but, nonetheless, justifiable. The broader conclusion, though, is that the overwhelming majority of laws that are retroactive in form are unjustifiable.

The rest of the book examines the history of Anglo-American attempts to address the problem of retroactive legislation. Generally, Anglo-American law has sought to deal with this issue in two ways. First, if at all possible, courts have tried to avoid the problem. Unless a statute expressly stated an intention to apply to pre-enactment transactions, courts traditionally applied the "presumption of prospectivity." Under this ancient presumption, lawmakers are presumed to intend statutes to apply prospectively. Although effective in cases of ambiguity, this presumption does not actually constrain the legislature's power to adopt retroactive legislation, if it does so in clear terms.

Second, if the legislature had adopted a clearly retroactive law, courts often invalidated the legislative action on constitutional grounds, relying either on express constitutional provisions or on the ground that such a law was beyond the power of the legislature. The Constitution's best known bars to retroactive lawmaking are, of course, the ex post facto clauses. These clauses, which expressly apply to both the federal and the state governments, provide that "no . . . *ex post facto* Law shall be passed."[8] Their companion provisions, the bill of attainder clauses, prohibit state legislatures and Congress from punishing particular individuals or classes of individuals for past behavior.

Other constitutional constraints on retroactive laws include the contracts, takings, and due process clauses. Article I, section 10 of the Constitution bans state passage of "any . . . law impairing the Obligation of Contracts."[9] The Fifth Amendment ensures that private property shall not "be taken for public use, without just compensation." And the due process clauses, of course, guarantee that life, liberty, and property shall not be deprived without due process of law.

At least since the New Deal era, most of these constraints on the power of the legislature to adopt retroactive laws—particularly the contract, takings, and due process clauses—have been narrowly construed. In some cases, the narrowing interpretations are of far more veritable origin. Most notably, few nonlawyers know that the ex post facto clauses have been construed since the early part of the nineteenth century as applying to criminal sanctions only. The bill of attainder clauses, which have not been used by the Supreme Court to invalidate a law since 1965, guard against only the most egregious invasions of personal liberty.

Thus, the current legal regime affords relatively meager constitutional protections against retroactive legislation. Moreover, especially since the 1960s and until a recent revival, courts had been diluting the presumption of prospectivity. Basically, since the New Deal era, the American legal system has overvalued change and given short shrift to settled expectations.[10] A revival of the defenses against retroactive legislation, which is discussed in chapter 10, is necessary to guard against further erosion of property rights, which are most often the target of retroactive laws.

When Is Legislation Retroactive?

For at least two reasons, deciding whether a law is or is not retroactive can be quite difficult.[11] The first reason is that, given the retrospective nature of almost all legislation, affixing the label "retroactive" to a law is a question of degree and requires balancing the authority of an earlier legislature against that of a later one. To illustrate: assume that Congress were to determine that all FCC licenses should run for twenty-year terms. Next assume that the subsequent Congress were to decide that the twenty-year terms held by existing licensees are too long, and that it wants to reclaim the spectrum faster, so that it may auction off that spectrum. The second Congress therefore proposes to limit existing licensees to five-year terms. The conflict between the preferences of the first and second Congresses in this hypothetical case may be called, in Professor Julian Eule's phrase, an "intertemporal conflict of laws" between the pronouncements of an earlier legislature and those of a later legislature.[12]

Eule properly notes that if the first Congress's decision is treated as immutable, we deny the next Congress the ability to implement its own views of proper public policy. In one sense, this is unremarkable—a later Congress must always deal with the world as it finds it, based in part on what past Congresses have done. Our system of government is not a pure democracy, where the peoples' representatives can radically reshape the law, and rights created under that law, as soon as they come into power. This conflict illustrates, though, that the concept of immutability, which Eule calls entrenchment, and the power to adopt retroactive laws "lie along a single time line. At some juncture, a prohibition against retroactivity becomes entrenching."[13]

The second problem with many of the classic definitions is that they fail to distinguish between retroactive laws and illegitimate laws. These definitions often conflate the definitional and normative questions mentioned above and wield the term "retroactive" as a pejorative conclusion, assuming that a retroactive law is per se illegitimate. To illustrate, writing "on circuit" in 1814, Joseph Story provided the classic statement on statutory retroactivity. In *Society for Propagating the Gospel v. Wheeler*,[14] he defined a law as retroactive where it "takes away or impairs vested rights acquired under existing law, or creates a new obligation, imposes a new duty, or attaches a new disability in respect to transactions or considerations already past." (The vexing problem of when a right is "vested" will be considered later.)[15]

Almost from the moment of Story's pronouncement, commentators have sought to understand and apply it. For example, one nineteenth-century lawyer defined a retroactive law as one "which changes or injuriously affects a present right by going behind it and giving efficiency to anterior circumstances to defeat it, which they had [not] when the right accrued."[16]

Neither of these classical definitions, however, clarifies the problem of differentiating between prospective laws, which almost inevitably have a retrospective effect, and retroactive laws. To illustrate, Professor Bryant Smith early in this century described a retrospective law as one that "extinguishes or impairs legal rights already acquired by the individual under the laws previously existing."[17] But, as noted, a prospective tax increase can be said to "impair legal rights" just as a law changing the terms of contracts currently in effect, which would surely be considered an illegitimately retroactive law.

That retrospectivity is a question of degree does not mean, however, that we cannot identify categories of laws that are unambiguously retroactive. Laws can be usefully divided into two basic categories, each having two subcategories.

Retroactive Laws. Retroactive laws are all those that explicitly refer to, and change the past legal consequences of, past behavior. Such laws can, in turn, be classified into two subcategories. The first type of retroactive law, which might be labeled *strongly retroactive*, consists of laws that are, on the face of the statute, "effective" even before the date of their enactment.[18] Such laws are easy to identify, and most often come up in the tax context. For example, Jerry Carlton was an estate's executor who in 1986 responded to a tax deduction that Congress had specifically created to encourage people to sell a company's stock to that company's employee stock ownership plan (ESOP). Mr. Carlton sold the stock to the ESOP for a loss, in order to get the benefit of the tax deduction. Congress then not only repealed the deduction, but also applied that repeal retroactively, costing the estate more than $600,000.[19] Such strongly retroactive laws are easy to identify, and are highly offensive. Indeed, they are so obviously offensive that, outside the tax context, legislatures do not often pass them.

A second subcategory of retroactive laws are those that operate forward from the date of enactment but explicitly make reference to, and change the legal consequences of, acts that took place in the past. These can be labeled *weakly retroactive* laws. Weakly retroactive laws operate forward but explicitly change the consequences of past behavior. The best example is the so-called Superfund law, which Congress passed in 1980 to deal with hazardous waste sites, as it has been interpreted by the courts. This law, officially known as the Comprehensive Environmental Response Compensation and Liability Act (CERCLA),[20] can impose massive retroactive liability on individuals or companies who generated, delivered, or owned waste that is found at a contaminated site. Courts have also interpreted CERCLA as establishing a strict liability scheme.[21] As one Superfund scholar describes it, this means that potentially responsible parties, known as PRPs, are "retroactively liable for the disposal of hazardous waste that took place thirty years earlier, even if the disposal was done in a 'state of the art' manner that was consistent with applicable laws."[22]

A forerunner of CERCLA was the Federal Coal Mine Health and Safety Act of 1969.[23] That act required mine operators to compensate certain miners, former miners, and their survivors for death or total disability caused by pneumoconiosis, so-called black lung disease. Mine owners had to pay this compensation even if the miners had left their employ years before the implementation of the act.

An oft-cited example helps to distinguish between strongly and weakly retroactive laws. Assume that a law was retroactively to validate a previously invalid marriage. If that law operates as if the new rule had always been the law and the affected marriage, as a result, is considered valid from its inception, then the law is strongly retroactive. If the marriage is deemed valid only as of the date of the law's enactment, it is weakly retroactive. This book will use the label "retroactive" to refer to both categories of laws; if it explicitly refers to the past, it is retroactive.

The only type of strongly or weakly retroactive laws that generally are justified are "curative" laws. Such legislation is designed to restore what was believed to be the status quo. Curative legislation serves many of the same values as a limitation on retroactive lawmaking—most notably, protecting expectations—and has generally been upheld by courts.[24] To illustrate, consider a law providing that a marriage is lawful only if the marriage certificate has affixed to it a special stamp, provided by the state. Suppose, as a result of a breakdown at the state printing office, these stamps are not ready when the law goes into effect. This stamp requirement is not well known, and people get married without having their certificate stamped. Few would object to legislation conferring validity on these otherwise-void marriages, even though such a law would unquestionably be retroactive.[25] Other than this category of laws, though, it is hard to conceive of a legitimate justification for either strongly or weakly retroactive legislation.

Retrospective Laws. Laws affecting past events, which is to say almost all laws, will be referred to as retrospective.[26] Such laws can be divided into two categories as well. The most difficult category of laws to classify and deal with are laws that do not mention prior events but that change the legal consequences of such events. Such legislation is *impliedly retroactive*. Claims that a law is impliedly retroactive will most often arise in the application of a law of general applicability to past events.

To illustrate, imagine a law providing a defense in future contract actions to all those who claim that they did not read an agreement. Such a law is prospective and presumably valid with respect to an individual who enters into an agreement after the law has been passed. Once this law has been passed, contracting parties are on notice that they must ensure that their contracting partner has actually read the agreement.

But what about the individual who entered into an agreement before this law was passed? Although the law may not expressly refer to past events, applying this law to parties who acted in the past under a different legal regime raises serious questions of fairness. The presumption of prospectivity is most helpful in dealing with this (large) category of laws. By assuming that the law was intended to be applied prospectively only, even if the law does not say so explicitly, adherence to this presumption wards off many close questions.

The remaining class of laws—into which almost every law falls—is ostensibly "prospective" laws. As noted, these laws may upset settled, investment-backed expectations, although they do not change the legal consequences of past actions.

This rule-based approach is akin to, and builds on, Justice Antonin Scalia's definition of retroactivity. Scalia distinguishes between what he calls "primary" and "secondary" retroactivity, which roughly correlate with the categories of retroactive and retrospective laws noted above. The example he provides is instructive:

> The Treasury Department might prescribe, for example, that for the purposes of assessing future income tax liability, income from certain trusts that has previously been considered non-taxable will be taxable—whether those trusts were established before or after the effective date of the regulation. That is not retroactivity in the sense at issue here, i.e., in the sense of altering the *past* legal consequences of past actions. Rather, it is what has been characterized as "secondary" retroactivity. . . . A rule with exclusively future effect (taxation of future trust income) can unquestionably *affect* past transactions (rendering the previously established trusts less desirable in the future).[27]

In a later case, Scalia expanded on this definition, stating that "the critical issue . . . is not whether the rule affects 'vested rights,' or governs substance or procedure, but rather what is the relevant activity that the rule regulates."[28] Professor Nelson Lund explains that

> under this approach, a statute imposing new substantive obligations . . . would be considered retroactive if it applied to conduct predating the statute's enactment. A statute establishing a new rule of evidence, however, regulates the conduct of trials; it would therefore be considered retroactive only if applied to evidence previously admitted or excluded from a trial.[29]

This distinction is worth noting because of its proper focus on a change to the "*past* legal consequences of past actions" and on whether the individual relied on the prior rule.[30] But the category of "secondary" retroactivity is often not helpful, in that almost every law "affects past transactions."

The alternative to the rule-based approach described above is generally a multifactor analysis that empowers courts to define and, presumably, under certain circumstances, invalidate legislation that goes too far. For example, Professor Jill Fisch recently proposed in the *Harvard Law Review* that legislation be invalidated as unfairly retroactive if it upsets a "stable" equilibrium. Her preferred approach would be that "if a rule has persisted over time, if it has been applied in a range of cases, and if its contours have been set by a high rulemaking authority, then the rule is more difficult to change."[31]

Fisch acknowledges that "these factors do not establish a bright-line rule."[32] She views this as a strength of her analysis, because retroactivity, she claims, is not binary but rather a question of degree, and because a rule-based approach follows "arbitrarily precise criteria."[33] She also rejects the type of rule-based formulation stated above because "it relies on a conception of legal rights or obligations that predates the adoption of a legal change without specifying where this conception comes from."[34]

Other commentators also suggest a similar, balancing-type of inquiry in assessing whether legislation is unlawfully retroactive. For example, Professor Charles Hochman urged courts to focus on "the strength and nature of the public interest served by the statute, the extent to which the statute modifies or abrogates the asserted preenactment right, and the nature of the right which the statute alters."[35]

A full defense of a rule-based approach over balancing tests and multifactor analyses is beyond the scope of this volume.[36] Suffice it to say that rule-based approaches, although they certainly do not eliminate all close questions, more narrowly constrain the discretion of judges. They also increase predictability, uniformity, and legitimacy.[37] Thus, such an approach is preferable to the more open-ended balancing tests.

The Increased Interest in Retroactivity

The problem of defining when laws are and are not retroactive, and when they should and should not be permitted, is of ancient origin. Many books and law review articles address this issue, and the number of Supreme Court and other judicial decisions that assess legislation with some retroactive effect is far too great to be comprehensively surveyed and collected.

A renewed inquiry into this problem is appropriate, however, for a few reasons. First, skepticism about government and about legal change has increased. Public choice theory has taught us, as Jonathan Macey has written, that legal changes are frequently the result of a process by which rules "seek to effectuate wealth transfers from societal groups that possess relatively little political power to other, more powerful, groups and coalitions."[38] This skepticism has led to justifiable mistrust of retroactive lawmaking.

Second, during President Clinton's first year in office, he proposed, and Congress adopted, retroactive tax increases. Although signed on August 10, 1993, these increases applied retroactively to January 1, 1993.[39] This event, which outraged many, has spurred renewed interest in this subject.

In fact, the recent memory of this tax has actually led to some congressional action to limit retroactive tax hikes. Most notably, at the beginning of the 104th Congress, the House of Representatives passed an internal rule declaring retroactive tax increases out of order.[40] Senator Paul Coverdell pushed a similar bar through a Senate committee.[41] Another proposal, the Common Sense Legal Reforms Act of 1995, would require the committee report on any legislation "of a public character" to specify "the retroactive applicability, if any, of that bill or joint resolution."[42]

Third, to the best of my knowledge, no article has comprehensively sought to tell the story of the two separate but related lines of legal authority that are necessary to understand the issue of retroactivity in the context of American law—the principle of prospectivity and the constitutional constraints on retroactive lawmaking.

The book's ultimate conclusion is that, although there may be cases where it is hard to define whether the application of a statute is retroactive, retroactive legislation is almost always unfair. For this reason, Congress should establish mechanisms making quite difficult the adoption of retroactive laws, especially those that would explicitly change the past legal consequences of past behavior. Courts, in turn, should ensure that statutes are applied retroactively only when Congress has expressly provided, after careful consideration, that the applicability of its new rule should turn on past conduct. Procedural mechanisms, plus a judicial clear-statement rule, will ensure that fewer retroactive laws are passed and that no law is treated as retroactive in the absence of a considered decision that it should be so applied. Courts should also more vigorously enforce the Constitution's takings and contracts clauses to ensure that the legislature does not "overconsume" retroactive legislation.

More important still is that a political consensus be forged against all retrospective legislation. Politicians should be encouraged to adopt truly prospective legislation only, and to make greater use of delayed effective dates and "grandfathering." Some of this consensus already exists and is embodied in the Constitution. As the framers well understood, the need for stability counsels in favor of making the act of legislating difficult.[43]

This consensus has to be reinvigorated, however. The case against retrospective legislation should not be hard to make: everyone understands the unfairness of changing the rules in the middle of the game. But only if retrospective legislation is made an issue, and if politicians are held politically accountable for such legislation when they approve it, can the incidence of such legislation be dramatically diminished.

In sum, the issue of retrospective legislation squarely presents the need to balance stability and flexibility. Enamored of change, our legal system has for the past few decades insufficiently understood the importance of providing notice and protecting reliance interests.

Limitations on Scope

To focus on the problem posed by the retroactive application of legislation affecting civil and property rights and interests, it has been necessary to limit the scope of this monograph. Most important, this book does not address the retroactive effect of judicial decisions, even though courts unquestionably engage in retrospective lawmaking—most notably, when they proclaim a new rule in the course of adjudication. In that circumstance, there is a serious potential for unfairness to the party who is subjected to that new rule. As one legal luminary put it earlier in this century, "The courts, with the consent of the state, have been constantly in the practice of applying in the decision of controversies rules which are not in existence . . . when the causes of controversy occurred. . . . Courts are constantly making *ex post facto* laws."[44]

In adjudication, however, retrospective decisions are unavoidable.[45] Every decision by a court, like every adjudicatory determination by an administrative agency, is explicitly a determination about past conduct. Litigation arises only when there is a substantial disagreement about (1) the law that existed at the time governing a past activity or (2) the nature of the activity—that is, a factual dispute. Those adjudicating a dispute peer into the past and determine that one was right and the other was wrong.

In most cases, the application of a new rule in adjudication will not raise serious questions of unfairness. Unlike statutes, which frequently rework entire areas of the law, most changes in judicial doctrine are evolutionary. Thus, parties are rarely surprised by the announcement of an entirely new and unanticipated rule. Evolutionary changes are easier to anticipate and plan for than are dramatic, revolutionary legal changes. In a sense, there is more notice of such a shift. And to the extent one believes the Blackstonian notion that the law is found rather than made,[46] the imposition by a court of a new rule on a (surprised) party can be justified.

The retrospective nature of judicial decision making is not only inevitable, it is also desirable, in that it constrains courts. In fact, during some years of the activist Warren Court, headed by Chief Justice Earl Warren, the Supreme Court routinely promulgated entirely new rules.[47] As a result, to avoid the massive dislocations and unfairness that would have attended retroactive application of some of these new rules, the Supreme Court began assessing on a case-by-case basis whether a new rule should be applied prospectively rather than retroactively.[48] Had the Court been unable to adopt such a case-by-case approach, it might not have been so quick to engage in judicial legislation. The cost would have been too great, for example, to free every criminal jailed in violation of a new procedural requirement that the Warren Court had concocted.

Thus, although the power to engage in retroactive lawmaking empowers legislatures, it constrains judges. This monograph therefore rejects the approach, suggested by Fisch, that adjudicative and legislative actions be analyzed together, since "both courts and legislators can control the temporal range of their lawmaking."[49] Retroactive lawmaking by courts is inevitable and, to a certain extent, desirable. The same cannot be said about retroactive legislation.

The debate about the power of courts to, in Fisch's terms, "control the temporal range of their lawmaking" also seems settled at this point. Recently, the U.S. Supreme Court adopted a firm rule that *all* its decisions are to be applied retroactively.[50] It is now clear that

> when the Court applies a rule of federal law to the parties
> before it, that rule is the controlling interpretation of federal

law and must be given full retroactive effect in all cases still open on direct review and as to all events, regardless of whether such events predate or postdate [the Court's] announcement of the rule.[51]

The Court has made clear that the "selective application of new rules" is no longer followed.[52] Thus, because adjudication is retroactive by necessity, and because the rules governing the retroactive effect of adjudicative decisions are clear, this volume does not address retroactive adjudication.

In addition, this volume does not deal at length with the issue of retroactive decision making by administrative agencies, which combine legislative and judicial functions.[53] In general, the ability of an administrative agency to promulgate retroactive rules via formal notice-and-comment rule making is analyzed in the same way that an act of Congress with retrospective effect is assessed. Absent an express statutory grant, administrative agencies are presumed to lack the authority to adopt rules retroactively.[54] Thus, to the extent that agencies act as delegatees of Congress in making rules, many of the same considerations discussed below apply to agency decisions with retroactive effect. Where agencies act like courts and engage in retrospective decision making in the course of adjudication, their activities are, for the reasons mentioned above, beyond the scope of this book.[55]

Finally, although the primary (but not exclusive) focus of this book is on retroactive lawmaking by Congress, it is worth noting that some states, such as New Hampshire, Colorado, Georgia, Idaho, Missouri, Ohio, Tennessee, and Texas, explicitly and unqualifiedly ban retroactive legislation.[56]

Part One

HISTORICAL ANTIPATHY TO RETROACTIVE LEGISLATION

2

MORAL AND ECONOMIC ARGUMENTS AGAINST RETROACTIVE LEGISLATION

Retroactive laws offend for both moral and practical reasons. Those who defend retroactive legislation give short shrift to property rights, expectation interests, and the ability of humans to make informed choices.

Moral Arguments against Retroactivity

The rules generated by a legal system have legitimacy only if that system is just. Retroactive laws are generally perceived by our society as unjust. This perception rests on our everyday experience. From early on, we learn not to change the rules in the middle of the game. We protest if our parents punish us without warning. We quickly come to dread unwelcome surprises. We expect warnings before dramatic events upset our expectations. And we mold our conduct based on the laws as we know and understand them.

　　Our culture manifests this expectation in many ways. The New Testament teaches that "Where no law is, there is no transgression."[1] As noted, self-improvement books repeatedly emphasize the importance of choosing a principle, sticking with it, and providing notice before changing it.

This idea of notice and of not applying rules *post hoc* is embedded in our fundamental law. As Oliver Wendell Holmes observed in *The Common Law*:

> But while the law is thus continually adding to its specific rules, it does not adopt the coarse and impolitic principle that a man always acts at his peril. On the contrary, its concrete rules, as well as the general questions addressed to the jury, show that the defendant must have had at least a fair chance of avoiding the infliction of harm before he becomes answerable for such a consequence of his conduct.[2]

Plainly, a defendant has not had, in Holmes's terms, "a fair chance of avoiding the infliction of harm" if no notice has been given him of the consequences of his conduct.

The concept of notice is fundamental to fairness and to the rule of law. A retroactive law is unfair precisely because it does not afford the affected individual notice about the rule that will be applied. As Benjamin Cardozo said, "law as a guide to conduct is reduced to the level of mere futility if it is unknown and unknowable."[3] Thus, when John Locke spoke of law in a civil society, he referred to "settled standing laws."[4] Or, as Dean Ronald Cass wrote, "a critical aspect of the commitment to a rule of law . . . is the premise that the government's force will be brought to bear on individuals—especially in criminal proceedings where that force is at its most fearsome—only after fair warning."[5]

The requirement that people be given notice of the legal implications of their behavior assumes that humans are, at least in part, moral actors, possessing free will.[6] It further assumes that we are capable not only theoretically of modifying our behavior depending on the rule of law, but that we do so in fact. Were we incapable of making choices, such that our behavior was unaffected no matter what the prevailing rule of law, then notice of the content of that rule would be irrelevant.[7]

If human beings were not capable of moral choice, or if they functioned without regard to the rule of law, then it would be irrational *not* to apply rule changes retroactively. To illustrate, suppose experience were to teach that a particular tax exemption ended up "costing" far more than was anticipated, thus increasing the budget deficit. If those who had structured their financial transactions to take advantage of that exemption would have made the exact same investment choices anyway, then that exemption should, rationally, be rescinded retroactively. But it is precisely because we cannot know whether the former assumption is true that retroactive changes in the law are considered unfair. In fact, experience teaches us that the tax exemption probably *did* influence the affected individual's investment decision.[8] Retroactive lawmaking thus contradicts our understanding of human beings as possessing free will or, at a minimum, as instrumentally rational creatures who change behavior in response to stimuli, including legal sanctions.

Notice is therefore fundamental to the rule of law, and not just for the reason that people are entitled to fair notice before the state subjects them to its power. Social order requires reliance.[9] Even a slave must be able to rely on a correlation between his own good behavior and his master's response. Without this correlation, there is no incentive to obey the master's commands. If the subjects of a state were to believe that the laws will be applied to them in a wholly arbitrary fashion, their incentive to comply with the law would evaporate. Thus, avoiding retroactive legislation increases individuals' incentives to conform their behavior to the law, and enhances the legitimacy of the legal system.

Practical Arguments against Retroactivity

There is another, more practical argument against retroactive legislation. As Professor Bryant Smith noted, retroactive laws, far more so than laws that apply prospectively, "may be passed with a knowledge of the precise conditions to which they are to apply and of the persons or classes on whom they will fall whatever burdens they may impose. They expose the lawgiver to greater temptation to partiality and corruption."[10] Smith put it another way: "a law for the future is impersonal; whereas a law for the past may be personal."[11] While some have argued that we are wiser in retrospect, a moral legal system should take account of the Hayekian critique that we often are not as wise as we think we are.[12] The nature of the rule of law is to substitute rules announced in advance for the judgment of men, particularly *post hoc*.

In accordance with this notion of the rule of law, the power to judge and punish people for past acts is limited to those institutions that we deem less likely to be partial. As Nelson Lund has aptly noted, "the authority to impose liability for completed conduct is a dangerous tool in the hands of politically responsive institutions."[13] By contrast, judicial rules are, at least in theory, created by a disinterested, apolitical body. This difference, as Professor Slawson says, ostensibly "diminishes the chance that prejudice or other irrational factors will control the decision."[14]

Also, unlike judges, who under the Constitution are confined to adjudicating the cases or controversies brought to them, legislatures can set their own agenda. This power to adopt wide-ranging retroactive laws is quite dangerous.

Legislatures are subject to influence and capture by special interest groups. If retroactive legislation is permitted, a group that has "lost" a struggle for resources will have a powerful incentive to try to undo that loss in the legislature. If those that would pay the costs of that reallocation are not as clearly defined or as well organized as the afflicted group, the likelihood is high that the legislature will respond to that afflicted group, at substantial cost to the public interest.

Economic Arguments against Retroactivity

Retroactive legislation imposes economic costs on society by undermining predictability, or the ability to rely on expectations. As Gregory Sidak and Daniel Spulber note, "expectations determine decisions and actions in a market economy."[15] If expectations are ignored, predictability is gone. Yet, as Cass points out, predictability "allows adjustments of individual behavior that increase societal well-being; increased predictability lowers costs associated with a decision."[16] Retroactive legislation thus leads to erroneous and therefore inefficient value assessments.[17]

Predictability is essential to continuing investments in productive enterprises, as well as to the availability of insurance. Decisions whether to invest or to provide insurance rely on the probabilities of a loss and the potential range of such loss. Retroactive legislation undercuts this vital predictability, expanding the range of possible outcomes, thus harming society by suppressing investment.

Stated another way, retroactive legislation is a contingency for which it is very difficult, if not impossible, for a firm to plan. Such legislation almost defines opportunistic behavior by the government. Fear of post-investment opportunism by the government may well deter parties from relying on the government's promises as much as they should for the sake of efficiency. That fear would be heightened with respect to investments in assets that are most valuable in one specific setting or relationship.[18]

To illustrate, a firm might invest less than would be optimal in a particular plant, if it fears that the government will revoke the plant's license to operate, or will impose impediments to the distribution of product from that plant. Fearful of being held up by the government, a firm will, *ex ante*, invest less than it optimally should. Alternatively, rational economic actors will demand higher returns on their riskier investments. Thus, the individual actors may not be harmed by such legislation, having factored that risk into their investment. But society would still be harmed, because the net amount of investment in such a society would be less than that which is optimally efficient.

Uncertainty as to operative rules discourages capital investment, which can be amortized only over time. To give an extreme example, few companies are willing to invest in a country where their permission to operate may be revoked at any time, and their property nationalized. Countries in which such governmental decisions have occurred have experienced a net decline in foreign investment.[19]

Pablo Spiller, who has extensively documented this phenomenon in developing countries, makes clear that "if the country's safeguarding institutions (*e.g.*, stable politics, independent judiciary, high growth rate, tradition of independent and professional regulatory agencies) are not sufficient to reduce the risk of administrative expropriation, then private investments in sectors with large economies of scale and sunk investments producing mostly for the local market will not be forthcoming."[20] The easiest way for the government to expropriate a firm's sunk investments is via retroactive legislation. Thus, limiting or precluding this device is apt to increase, or at least to create the conditions for increased, investment.

Even a law that may be inefficient as a matter of social welfare may be "efficient" if it is well specified and known in advance. At the very least, such a law permits the parties to arrange their affairs accordingly, thus maximizing social welfare within the constraints of the law (that is, they can minimize the law's costs).

Defenders of Retroactive Laws

Some scholars believe that retroactive laws should not—and cannot—be analyzed differently from other laws. Their arguments can be summarized as follows:

• *Circularity*. The argument against retroactive legislation is circular, these scholars maintain. If everyone understood at the outset that their expectations could be upset, these critics contend, then there would be no settled expectations, and therefore nothing would be wrong with retroactive legislation.[21]

• *Similarity.* As has been noted, both laws that are nominally prospective and laws that are nominally retroactive can upset expectations.[22] Any differences in impact between nominally prospective and retrospective laws are differences in degree and not in kind.[23] Given that retroactive laws raise the same issues as other laws, some contend, there is no reason to distinguish between retroactive and other laws. Also, because the differences are of degree, no precise definitions of retroactive laws are possible.

• *No economic difference.* Retroactive rules do not necessarily cost more than prospective laws. As Fisch points out, "a rule that retroactively imposes a million dollars in liability for past pollution activities has the same wealth effect as the nominally prospective adoption of stricter emissions controls that reduce the value of the manufacturer's factory by a million dollars."[24]

• *More efficient lawmaking.* Efficient lawmaking—that is, lawmaking that maximizes the net benefits of legal change—favors retroactive laws. As Fisch says, this notion is "based on the utilitarian conception of a net gain in social welfare without regard for distributional issues."[25] The lack of regard for distributional issues means that, although there is a net social gain, there are also identifiable winners and losers when a law is applied retroactively.[26]

• *The distinction is based on a fiction.* It is a fiction that people "know the law." Since most laws are applied without actual notice, which is the fundamental complaint about retroactive laws, why should retroactive laws be treated differently?

Although many of these arguments have force, ultimately they must be rejected. Taking these objections in order, the circularity argument presumes that there are no preexisting property rights and other reliance interests—that is, that they are the creation of government. To state the extreme version of this argument, no one will expect to hold property if they are told that all property is subject to confiscation at any time. Such an argument is of dubious constitutional validity. The Constitution both presumes and protects private property rights. It is beyond the power of government to define out of existence all expectation interests.

Second, although it is true that the differences between retroactive and retrospective laws are generally of degree, the legal system can and often does address such differences. To quote Lon Fuller, "as with other desiderata that make up the internal morality of the law, difficulties and nuances should not blind us to the fact that, while perfection is an elusive goal, it is not hard to recognize blatant indecencies."[27] The presence of close questions cannot shut down the enterprise.

There are key differences between prospective and retroactive legislation. Prospective legislation destroys the status quo, on which people rely in making everyday decisions, less often and to a lesser extent than do retroactive laws. Retroactive lawmaking is more unusual, thereby coming as a greater surprise.[28] Also, even if prospective legislation disrupts settled expectations, such laws generally offer a way out before imposing new liability. As Dean Cass has pointed out,

> the distinction between retrospective and prospective decisions is important precisely because the effects of one are less binding. A penalty of any given magnitude is more threatening—in terms of its capacity to interfere with personal autonomy, disrupt existing plans, undermine settled expectations, and impose greater disutility on those whose plans and property are changed—when it is less easily evaded.[29]

To address the third argument, although the direct economic costs of retroactive and prospective laws may be the same, retroactive costs impose greater transition costs. A society in which retroactive legislation is routine will experience less investment than is economically efficient.

There are also important psychological differences between retroactive and prospective laws. Retroactive laws frequently remove benefits currently enjoyed, while prospective rules may cause opportunities to be forgone. This may be all the same as an economic matter, but every child knows the difference between the experience of having a toy taken away and that of not being given an additional toy.[30] At a minimum, the child deserves fair notice before being told that he or she will have to share the toy. Only if the child were given the toy illegally—for example, if his parent had stolen it—should the child's feelings be subordinated to the social need to uphold the rule of law. Failing to take these psychological effects into account can imperil the legitimacy of the legal regime.

Fourth, the argument that retroactive lawmaking is more efficient lawmaking assumes that legal change is positive and evolutionary. Public choice theory teaches us that legal change is often harmful, however. It is also precisely the efficiency of retroactive laws in allowing a legislature to target winners and losers that can make such legislation unfair and potentially draconian.

Fifth, although it is certainly true that no one can know all of the law, people are aware of their legal obligations as a general matter. Drivers may not know every provision of the traffic code, but they know enough to understand in most circumstances what is right and wrong. In fact, there is no choice but to assume that people know the law, both for the application of the criminal law and to avoid accepting a principle that would allow all laws to be changed arbitrarily. And where individuals have a particular interest in a matter, they are more likely to know the law.

Most fundamentally, those who defend retroactive legislation need to articulate forceful reasons why the need for legal change is so important that it should override the fairness concerns created by retroactive legislation. Those defending untrammeled change must explain why such extreme (and compensated) change is a positive good. Although those attacking retroactivity analysis have highlighted flaws in that analysis, they have not explained why the entire enterprise should be abandoned.

The defenders of retroactive lawmaking fail to realize that restrictions on such lawmaking do not preclude legal change. They moderate it. To illustrate, the presumption of prospectivity guards against extreme legal change that thwarts settled expectations, in the absence of a clear societal (or, at the very least, legislative) consensus that such extreme change is necessary. The takings clause ensures that just compensation is paid for laws that upset such expectations. The contracts, ex post facto, bill of attainder, and due process clauses guard against particular applications of certain defined forms of legal change. The following chapters explore what has happened to dilute these restrictions on retroactive legislation and what can be done to revive them.

3

❖

THE RISE, FALL, AND RESURGENCE OF ANTIPATHY TO RETROACTIVITY

The primary means of dealing with legislation that could be construed as retroactive has been to avoid the problem, by indulging the presumption that legislation is intended to be applied prospectively. The basis for this presumption is, of course, hostility to legislation that unduly upsets legitimate, settled expectations. The force of this presumption has varied throughout American history, declining somewhat in the 1960s and 1970s. Recently it has made a comeback. Even the "strong" version of this presumption does not, however, prevent a determined legislature from adopting retroactive legislation.

Origins of the Presumption against Retroactivity

The hostility to retroactive legislation has deep roots. Ancient law, for example, stated that laws and customs should be applied to future transactions only; they could not be applied to past acts unless the laws expressly stated that they applied either to past time or to pending transactions.[1] Through Bracton, who included this rule in his influential 1250 treatise, this principle became part of the common law.[2] It was Lord Coke, though, who embodied the bias against retroactive legislation in a common-law maxim when he construed a statute as applying only prospectively, declaring: "For it is a rule and law of Parliament, that Regularly *Nova constitution futuris formam imponere debet non praeteritis"*—a new statute should govern the future, not the past.[3]

In practice, though, this principle was invoked only where a party was harmed by the retroactive operation of a statute; benefits could be granted retroactively. Thus, Coke stated that Acts of Parliament should not be construed to harm a person who was free from wrong.[4] Coke further maintained that a person was injured if the retroactive application of a law worked to his disadvantage. Even Coke's formulation, however, was subject to the doctrine of parliamentary supremacy.[5] A determined Parliament could pass a retroactive law if it said so clearly enough.

Blackstone's Injunction against Retroactivity

In describing the properties of "the municipal law," Sir William Blackstone highlighted the centrality of notice to the rule of law.[6] "A bare resolution," he said, "confined in the breast of the legislator, without manifesting itself by some external sign, can never be properly a law. It is requisite that this resolution be notified to the people who are to obey it."[7] For this reason, he concluded, "it is incumbent on the promulgators to [notify the public] in the most public and perspicuous manner, not like Caligula, who (according to Dio Cassius) wrote his laws in a very small character, and hung them upon high pillars, the more effectually to ensnare the people."[8] Blackstone continued:

> There is still a more unreasonable method than this, which is called making of laws *ex post facto*; when after an action is committed, the legislator then for the first time declares it to have been a crime, and inflicts a punishment on the person who has committed it; here it is impossible that the party could foresee that an action, innocent when it was done, should be afterwards converted to guilt by a subsequent law; he therefore had no cause to abstain from it; and all punishment for not abstaining must of consequence be cruel and unjust.[9]

He concluded: "All laws should be therefore made to commence *in futuro*, and be notified before their commencement; which is implied in the term 'prescribed.'"[10]

Blackstone profoundly influenced the American common law, the founding generation, and the Constitution.[11] Perhaps the greatest indication of Blackstone's influence is that Forrest McDonald, in his landmark work on the intellectual origins of the Constitution, considers Blackstone's view of English law and legal history—even when Blackstone was wrong—as the best evidence of what the framers thought. As McDonald says, "Modern scholarship has demonstrated that Blackstone was mistaken on a number of counts, but few if any Americans knew that, and it was Blackstone whom they read on the subject."[12]

Incorporation of the Principle into Early American Law

American law assimilated and amplified the hostility to retroactive legislation. The principle takes three relevant forms in early American law. First, American courts shared the common-law presumption against giving statutes retroactive effect. Second, the Constitution embodied certain substantive limits on the ability of even a determined legislature to adopt retroactive criminal legislation (the ex post facto clauses), federal laws that confiscated property without compensation (the takings clause), and state laws that impeded the obligations of contracts (the contracts clause). Third, there was some support for the notion that retroactive legislation, even if not plainly precluded by the text of the Constitution, could violate vested rights, which were protected under natural law, and thus was void.

The Supreme Court first addressed retroactive legislation in the landmark case of *Calder v. Bull*,[13] decided in 1798. This case is generally cited for the proposition that the ex post facto clause applies to criminal legislation only. This topic will be addressed below, in our consideration of the ex post facto clauses.[14] But *Calder* also sheds light on the presumption of prospectivity, and on the notion that natural law precluded retroactive legislation.

Calder involved a determination by the Connecticut legislature that a judicial decree should be set aside and a new trial held. Reviewing later state court proceedings, the Court agreed that the legislature's action was not a forbidden ex post facto law in violation of Article I, Section 10, of the Constitution. Justice Samuel Chase wrote the first opinion. After defining ex post facto laws, Chase stated that:

> Every *ex post facto* law must necessarily be retrospective; but every retrospective law is not an *ex post facto* law: The former, only, are prohibited. Every law that takes away, or impairs, rights vested, agreeably to existing laws, is retrospective, and is generally unjust; and may be oppressive; and it is a good general rule, that a law should have no retrospect; but there

are cases in which laws may justly, and for the benefit of the community, and also of individuals, relate to a time anteced-ent to their commencement; as statutes of oblivion, or of pardon.[15]

Thus, Chase contended that, although retroactive laws are gener-ally to be avoided where possible, the Constitution did not prohibit them in every case.

Chase also ignited a debate over the role of natural law in consti-tutional litigation that Professor David Currie says, with characteristic understatement, "never has simmered down completely."[16] Chase ar-gued that:

> [T]here are certain vital principles in our free republican gov-ernments, which will determine and overrule an apparent and flagrant abuse of legislative power. . . . An act of the legislature (for I cannot call it a law) contrary to the first great principles of the social compact, cannot be considered a rightful exercise of legislative authority.[17]

Given Chase's conclusion that the ex post facto clause did not apply to civil legislation, Currie properly understands this phrase as suggesting "that the reason Chase upheld the legislature's action was that it im-paired no vested right and therefore was consistent with natural jus-tice."[18] This "natural rights–vested rights" tradition, profoundly hostile to retroactive laws, is discussed at greater length below.[19]

From *Calder* through the rest of the nineteenth century and well into the twentieth, the Supreme Court adhered to a strong presump-tion against retroactive legislation. For example, the Supreme Court in 1806 refused to apply a new, and lower, commission rate for cus-toms collectors to amounts already bonded but not yet collected at the time the new rates took effect. The Court declared that the "words of a statute ought not to have a retrospective operation, unless they are so clear, strong, and imperative, that no other meaning can be an-nexed to them, or unless the intention of the legislature cannot other-wise be satisfied."[20] This tradition prevailed until the 1960s, even as a more hostile approach toward retroactive legislation rose and then fell.

A Natural Rights Tradition

Federal and state courts have treated retroactive laws as invalid on natural law grounds, without reference to or reliance on the Constitution. Under this view, even apart from constitutional limitations, the natural rights of man constrain the legislature's power to act. Although this "vested rights" mode of reasoning has fallen into disfavor in our time, it was much in evidence in the early nineteenth century.

Perhaps most well known is *Fletcher v. Peck*,[21] where the Supreme Court struck down, under the contracts clause, Georgia's repeal of a land grant. As an alternative ground for the decision, Chief Justice Marshall flirted with a natural law vested rights approach. Declaring that "it may well be doubted whether the nature of society and of government does not prescribe some limits to the legislative power," Marshall thought Georgia's action unconstitutional "either by general principles which are common to our free institutions, or by the particular provisions of the Constitution of the United States."

Almost as famous is Chancellor Kent's condemnation of retroactive legislation in *Dash v. Van Kleeck*,[22] in which a creditor sued a sheriff for allowing his debtor to escape from the sheriff's custody. After the creditor had filed his suit, the legislature adopted a statute providing the sheriff with a defense against such actions. That statute, however, failed to say if it should be applied retroactively or not. Kent, sitting on the New York Supreme Court, said it should not. He then proclaimed that the power of the legislature to adopt retroactive laws was limited:

> Our constitutions do not admit the power assumed by the Roman prince; and the principle we are now considering is regarded as sacred. It is not pretended that we have any express constitutional provision on the subject; nor have we any other for numerous other rights dear alike to freedom and to justice. An *ex post facto* law, in the strict technical sense of the term, is usually understood to apply to criminal cases, and this is its meaning when used in the Constitution of the United States; yet laws impairing previously acquired civil rights are equally within the reason of that prohibition and equally to be condemned. . . . [T]here is no distinction in principle, nor any recognized in practice, between a law punishing a person criminally, for a past innocent act, or punishing him civilly by divesting him of a lawfully acquired right. The distinction consists only in the degree of oppression.[23]

Less eloquently, in *Terrett v. Taylor*,[24] the U.S. Supreme Court held that the Constitution barred Virginia from revoking a long-existing land grant to the Episcopal church. Its mode of reasoning was spiced with natural law and vested rights rhetoric:

> But that the legislature can repeal statutes creating private corporations, or conforming to them property already acquired under the faith of previous laws . . . we are not prepared to admit; and we think ourselves standing upon *the fundamental laws of every free government*, upon the spirit and letter of the Constitution of the United States, and upon the decisions of the most respectable judicial tribunals, in resisting such a doctrine.[25]

In 1822 Justice Hosmer of the Connecticut Supreme Court declared that "the question, where no constitutional objection exists, whether the judiciary may void a retroactive law operating on vested rights, is undetermined."[26] Hosmer believed that the legislature was not omnipotent, even in the absence of constitutional restraints. He said, "Should there exist . . . a case of direct interaction on vested rights, too palpable to be questioned, and, too unjust to admit of vindication, I could not avoid considering it as a violation of the social compact, and within the control of the judiciary."[27]

Seven years later, unsuccessfully arguing against a retroactive law in *Wilkinson v. Leland*, Daniel Webster contended that "though there be no prohibition in the constitution, the legislature is restrained from committing flagrant acts, from acts subverting the great principles of republican liberty, and of the social compact; such as giving the property of A. to B."[28] This decision exemplifies the use of natural law rhetoric in the Supreme Court during this era. The case involved a challenge to legislation adopted by Rhode Island in 1792 to ratify title to some Rhode Island property. The contested piece of property had, in 1791, been sold to one Moses Brown and Oziel Wilkinson by an executrix of a will who had lacked the authority to make the sale. The rightful heirs, who lived in New Hampshire, contended that the act of the Rhode Island legislature could not retroactively wipe out their property rights.

The Supreme Court, with Justice Story, assumed that the New Hampshire heirs were correct in their statement of the law, and that a legislature could not "transfer the property of A. to B., without his consent."[29] No such act, Story declared, "has ever been held a constitutional exercise of power, in any state of the Union."[30] He upheld the law, however, on the grounds that the challenged legislation did not "divest the settled rights of property" because Brown and Wilkinson had purchased the land in good faith.[31] Thus, although the opinion is larded with statements about the inherent, natural law limitations on the power of legislatures, the decision actually *upholds* the legislation.

Story's treatise on constitutional law echoed his condemnation of retrospective laws in *Wilkinson v. Leland*:

> If such a law be void, it is upon principles derived from the general nature of free governments and the necessary limitations created thereby. . . . Whether, indeed, independently of the Constitution of the United States, the nature of republican and free governments does not necessarily impose some restraints on the legislative power has been much discussed. It seems to be the general opinion, fortified by a strong current of judicial opinion, that . . . no state government can be presumed to possess the transcendental sovereignty to take away vested rights of property; to take the property of A and transfer it to B by a mere legislative act.[32]

Echoing Story, one New York court in 1850 declared that the rights of parties rest "not merely on the Constitution, but upon the great principles of eternal justice which lie at the foundation of all free governments."[33]

As late as 1885, one prominent treatise, entitled *Dwarris on Statutes*, wrote:

> Laws must of necessity and from their nature, be prospective, otherwise they cannot be rules of civil conduct. Laws cannot attach themselves to conduct antecedent to the creation of the rules themselves. This would be a thing impossible for at the time the transaction took place, there being no rule, a law subsequently passed, was not, and from the nature of the case, could not have been an existing rule governing such transaction.[34]

It bears noting, though, as in the cases of *Fletcher v. Peck* and *Wilkinson v. Leland*, that this natural law notion was rarely the sole basis for court decisions. Frequently, courts would find that the legislature did not intend the law at issue to be retroactive, thus using the presumption of prospectivity to avoid making a constitutional decision. Alternatively, as in *Wilkinson*, a court would find that the law was permissible for another reason.[35] Thus Hochman is probably correct in concluding that "this natural law theory never attained widespread acceptance in the opinions of the Supreme Court, and it has long been accepted that retroactivity is a ground for holding a statute void only if it contravenes a specific provision of the Constitution."[36]

The Presumption in the U.S. Supreme Court before 1969

Thus, as noted, rather than invalidate a statute as unconstitutionally retroactive, particularly in the absence of a clear constitutional provision, courts would try to avoid the problem of retroactivity entirely by relying on the presumption of prospectivity. This maxim of statutory interpretation, which obviously reflected hostility to retroactive legislation, was often invoked in tandem with statements condemning the injustice of retroactivity. These statements led to the correlative assumption that, surely, the legislature could not have intended to undertake such a monstrous act as the passage of a retroactive law.

For example, in 1854, the U.S. Supreme Court in *Murray v. Gibson* refused to give retroactive application to a Mississippi statute that limited to three years the time in which another state court judgment would be enforced by Mississippi courts against a citizen of Mississippi.[37] The Court reaffirmed that "as a general rule for the interpretation of statutes, it may be laid down, that they never should be allowed a retroactive operation where this is not required by express command or by necessary and unavoidable implication. Without such command or implication they speak and operate in the future only."[38]

The strong presumption of prospectivity continued in ascendancy for more than a century. Justice Scalia has collected the following representative expressions of the "strong" presumption of prospectivity:[39]

- *White v. United States* (1903): "Where it is claimed that a law is to have a retrospective operation, such must be clearly the intention, evidenced in the law and its purposes, or the court will presume that the lawmaking power is acting for the future only and not for the past."[40]
- *United States Fidelity & Guaranty Co. v. United States ex rel. Struthers Wells Co.* (1908): "There are certain principles which have been adhered to with great strictness by the courts in relation to the construction of statutes as to whether they are or are not retroactive in their effect. The presumption is very strong that a statute was not meant to act retrospectively, and it ought never to receive such a construction if it is susceptible of any other. It ought not to receive such a construction unless the words used are so clear, strong and imperative that no other meaning can be annexed to them or unless the intention of the legislature cannot be otherwise satisfied."[41]

- *Union Pacific R. Co. v. Laramie Stock Yards Co.* (1913): "A retrospective operation will not be given to a statute which interferes with antecedent rights or by which human action is regulated, unless such be the unequivocal and inflexible import of the terms, and the manifest intention of the legislature."[42]
- *Schwab v. Doyle* (1922): "The initial admonition is that laws are not to be considered as applying to cases which arose before their passage unless that intention be clearly declared. . . . If the absence of such determining declaration leaves to the statute a double sense, it is the command of the cases that which rejects retroactive application must be selected."[43]
- *Miller v. United States* (1935): "A statute cannot be construed to operate retrospectively unless the legislative intention to that effect unequivocally appears."[44]

These examples may be multiplied many times over. But even as the strong presumption was the Court's major theme, a minor, dissonant theme was emerging.

Tax Cases—Increased Tolerance for Retroactivity

As the line of authority applying a strong presumption of prospectivity developed, so too did a later-arising, but parallel tradition more tolerant of retroactive legislation. In short, during the Progressive Era, Congress began imposing taxes retroactively and, by and large, the Supreme Court upheld them. As a result, most commentators recognize that the Supreme Court's "cases involving the retroactive imposition of taxes must be treated separately" from the cases reviewing other retroactive legislation.[45]

In the Revenue Act of 1913, Congress first enacted a general revenue statute with an effective date before the date of actual enactment.[46] It has done so many times since. Generally, the increased tax rate is applied retroactively to the beginning of the year in which the tax is adopted. But in 1918 and 1926, each of the Revenue Acts was applicable to the entire calendar year that had preceded enactment.[47]

At first the Court struck down retroactive gift tax statutes.[48] But in 1930 the Court upheld a capital gains tax passed in November 1921 that was made effective as of the beginning of 1921, and which had been challenged by a party who had sold stock before the legislation had been passed.[49] The next year, it upheld a tax under the same retroactive gift tax statute that it had invalidated eleven years earlier.[50]

This early experimentation with retroactivity was the proverbial camel's nose under the tent. Congress became accustomed to passing retroactive legislation that impinged on economic rights, and the Court became accustomed to upholding such laws. For example, in *Milliken v. United States*,[51] the Court established the doctrine that the existence of an estate tax at some rate was fair warning that the rates might be changed.

In 1935 one commentator, after considering the Supreme Court's cases and Congress's unchallenged habit of passing income tax laws retroactive to the beginning of the calendar year in which they were enacted, pronounced restrictions on the retroactive application of taxes "dead."[52]

Welch v. Henry, decided in 1938, proved him correct, both in its holding and in the Court's justification for routinely allowing the retroactive application of taxes.[53] In March of 1935, Wisconsin passed a law increasing certain taxes for 1933 and 1934. The challenger had filed his 1933 return, as required, in March of 1934. He objected to an increased tax on his income from corporate dividends in 1933. The Court rejected his claim, saying that:

> Taxation is neither a penalty imposed on the taxpayer nor a liability which he assumes by contract. It is a way of apportioning the cost of government among those who in some measure are privileged to enjoy its benefits and must share its burdens. Since no citizen enjoys immunity from that burden, its retroactive imposition does not necessarily infringe due process, and to challenge the present tax it is not enough to point out that the taxable event, the receipt of the income, antedated the tax.[54]

Paving the way for later retroactive tax increases that go back as far as *ten* years,[55] and rejecting an equal protection clause challenge, the Court in *Welch v. Henry* said that

> lapse of time did not remove that difference [of treatment from other classes of income] so as to compel equality of treatment when the income was taxed at a later date. . . . The equal protection clause does not preclude the legislature from changing its mind in making an otherwise permissible choice of subjects of taxation.[56]

Thus, vis-à-vis the retroactivity of tax increases, the situation today is identical to that described by the Supreme Court in 1937: "We may safely say that it is a customary congressional practice" to apply certain forms of tax legislation retroactively.[57] But the real legacy of these early tax cases was to set the stage for the toleration of other retroactive civil legislation that compromised settled, investment-backed expectations.

The Switch in Time

Throughout the Progressive Era, the Supreme Court faced pressure to uphold redistributive laws that dramatically increased the power of government. That pressure intensified, and began to have some effect, after the Great Depression. Although the metamorphosis of constitutional law spanned nearly a decade, the date most associated with that sea change is 1937. That year, shortly after Franklin Delano Roosevelt's Court-packing plan, Justice Owen Roberts began voting with those justices who sought to uphold New Deal legislation. His decision to do so spelled the end of the so-called *Lochner* era, as well as of the reign of the "Nine Old Men." After 1937, the Court began routinely upholding New Deal and other legislation affecting existing economic rights, and it has been doing so ever since.[58]

This "switch in time that saved nine" had implications for the presumption against retroactive legislation as well. As federal power grew, so too did the number of retroactive statutes. With the waning of substantive due process to protect economic rights, along with the validation of New Deal legislation, the Court became increasingly tolerant of explicitly retroactive legislation. Thus, according to William Eskridge and Philip Frickey, "Since the New Deal era, retroactive statutes have become quite common, and in the overwhelming majority of cases, they have withstood constitutional challenges."[59]

The Court continued, however, to interpret ambiguous statutes as applying prospectively only. Surveying the Court's practice on this subject, Scalia concluded that "during these more than 150 years of doctrinal certainty, . . . if the new law was silent as to its application, we consistently employed the presumption that it applied only prospectively."[60]

In short, from the 1930s through 1969, the Court was unwilling to invalidate retroactive legislation on contracts clause or substantive due process grounds. To take but one example, in *El Paso v. Simmons*,[61] the Court upheld Texas's decision to wipe out rights, previously granted to landowners, to reinstate their interests in lands by paying back interest.[62] Despite the Court's unwillingness to invalidate clearly retroactive laws, however, the Court continued to try to avoid the problem where possible by construing ambiguous statutes as applying prospectively. The Court's overt commitment to the antiretroactivity presumption was not compromised until the implications of Justice Roberts's 1937 "switch" were fully realized during the Warren Court era.

As late as 1964, the Supreme Court was still applying the presumption of prospectivity with force in cases of ambiguity. Thus, in *Greene v. United States*,[63] the Court found that a terminated Department of Defense employee's claim of wrongful termination had matured under a 1955 rule. The Court therefore held inapplicable a more restrictive 1960 regulation that had been adopted after the claim had arisen and been formally presented. The Court invoked "the first rule of construction" for agency regulations and statutes, holding that "retrospective operation will not be given to a statute which interferes with antecedent rights . . . unless such be the 'unequivocal and inflexible import of the terms, and the manifest intention of the legislature.'"[64]

The Court Takes a Wrong Turn

By the 1960s, Congress had been enacting retroactive statutes for a long time, and the Supreme Court had basically ceased invalidating them on constitutional grounds. This was certainly true in the tax area, but federal courts had also upheld the retroactive application of rent controls,[65] numerous legislative modifications to existing franchise (and other) contracts,[66] mortgage moratoriums,[67] reductions in the rights of municipal bondholders,[68] and other clear impairments of the right to contract.[69] Nonetheless, as noted above, the Supreme Court had essentially hewn to its strong presumption against the retroactive application of statutes absent an express indication to the contrary. Then, during the Warren Court era, as Lund has written:

> The Court occasionally began to ignore the presumption that statutes do not operate retroactively unless they expressly so provide, substituting for that principle a declaration that courts should ordinarily apply the law in effect at the time of the judicial decision.[70]

This development, as Lund reports, along with the Court's *prospective* application of some of its own normally retroactive decisions, "were side effects of the Court's increased willfulness, which often converted constitutional adjudication into a legislative process and statutory interpretation into ad hoc judicial policymaking."[71]

The Court's first dramatic departure from the presumption against retroactive legislation was in *Thorpe v. Housing Authority of Durham*.[72] *Thorpe* involved an attempt by the city of Durham, North Carolina, to evict a tenant from low-income housing. The tenant contended that her role in organizing a tenant's association caused the termination, and that this termination violated her First Amendment rights. The North Carolina Supreme Court rejected her claim, and the United States Supreme Court agreed to hear her case. While Ms. Thorpe's case was pending before the U.S. Supreme Court, the federal Department of Housing and Urban Development adopted a rule requiring that "before instituting an eviction proceeding local housing authorities . . . should inform the tenant . . . of the reasons for the eviction."[73] Without citing the presumption against retroactivity, the Court held that HUD's new regulation invalidated the eviction order, which had been issued almost eighteen months before the new rule had been instituted.

In so doing, the Supreme Court relied on its early decision in *The Schooner Peggy*.[74] That case had involved a treaty that had been signed while the case was on appeal and that had changed the law. Based on the treaty's change in the law, the Court reversed the lower court's decree. Invoking that decision, the *Thorpe* Court declared: "The general rule is that an appellate court must apply the law in effect at the time it renders its decision."[75]

Five years later, in *Bradley v. Richmond School Board*,[76] the Court further undercut the presumption against retroactivity. In *Bradley*, the Supreme Court held that a court of appeals should apply a statute providing for the award of attorney's fees that had been enacted while an appeal from the district court's award of fees was pending. Recalling its decision in *Thorpe*, among others, the Court "reject[ed] the contention that a change in the law is to be given effect in a pending case only where that is the clear and stated intention of the legislature."[77] Rather, the Court suggested that, absent an indication to the contrary, a new statute should be applied retroactively unless it would cause "manifest injustice."[78] The Court identified three relevant factors in assessing "manifest injustice:" (1) the nature and identity of the parties; (2) the nature of their rights; and (3) the nature of the effect of the change in law on those rights.[79]

As Justice Scalia demonstrated in his concurring opinion in *Kaiser Aluminum v. Bonjorno*, none of the decisions that *Thorpe* and *Bradley* rested on were "genuinely contrary to that generally applied presumption."[80] Scalia's detailed critique of *Thorpe* and *Bradley* in *Bonjorno* should have convinced the Court that it had made a mistake in departing from so well established a principle and in substituting a balancing test for a bright-line rule.[81] But, intent on doing "the right thing" in some individual cases, the Court had inaugurated a period of uncertainty with adverse consequences for the rule of law.

The Legacy of *Thorpe* and *Bradley*

Whatever the deficiencies in the Court's case analysis, *Thorpe* and *Bradley* had compromised the strong presumption against retroactivity. Thus in 1985, when the Court repeated Karl Llewellyn's famous point that there existed conflicting canons for and against the retroactive application of legislation, it was now essentially correct.[82] And it was during this period that Congress passed, and courts applied retroactively, a number of laws that probably would not have been given retroactive effect had the strong presumption of prospectivity remained in force. The prime example of this phenomenon is the Superfund program, the Comprehensive Environmental Response, Compensation, and Liability Act (CERCLA).

Even though *Thorpe* and *Bradley* had involved the adoption of a law during the course of an adjudication, the logical implications of the *Thorpe-Bradley* approach were far broader. As Professor William Luneberg has noted, "Predictably, courts have not viewed *Thorpe* as necessarily limited to situations where a new regulation takes effect during the litigation."[83]

During this time, the Court decided *Usery v. Turner Elkhorn Mining*,[84] one of the most often cited and discussed cases involving retroactivity. The case, alluded to above, involved Congress's power to adopt a statute requiring owners of coal mines to bear the expenses of their former employees who had contracted Black Lung disease. Unlike the case in *Thorpe* and *Bradley*, the statute at issue was not ambiguous; it was unquestionably retroactive. In *Usery*, the Court buried the already dead doctrine of substantive due process as a basis for combating retroactive laws, and it held that Congress did indeed have the authority to enact the legislation. After *Thorpe* and *Bradley*, and especially after *Turner*, courts no longer needed to use the principle of prospectivity to avoid potential constitutional problems because retroactive legislation did not appear to pose any such problem. Under *Turner*, legislatures seemed to have virtually plenary authority to adopt retroactive legislation.

The starkest example of the consequences of the *Thorpe-Bradley* misstep was in the interpretation of the Superfund program, CERCLA, a last-minute political compromise that one court has described as "marred by vague terminology and deleted provisions."[85] Section 107(a) of CERCLA provides that, subject to limited defenses, "any person who at the time of the disposal of any hazardous substance owned or operated any facility at which such hazardous substances were disposed of . . . shall be liable."[86] Liability also extends to generators who "arranged for" the disposal, treatment, or transportation of waste.

According to *Brown v. Georgeoff*, "[t]here are no unequivocal statements in the statute indicating a Congressional intent to make [section 107(a)] apply retroactively."[87] Nor was "the precise issue of retroactivity . . . addressed in the Congressional debates."[88] Nonetheless, relying on *Thorpe* and *Bradley*, courts accepted the Environmental Protection Agency's argument that the past tense of the phrase "arranged for" in Superfund meant that the statute should be applied to impose retroactive liability on all those who came within the statute's ambit for harms that happened before the statute's enactment.[89]

Applying this statute retroactively has dramatic implications. Companies that, at the time, had disposed of their hazardous waste in good faith, pursuant to law, sometimes even under a permit, have been slapped with what could be back-breaking liabilities.[90] The Congressional Budget Office released a report in January 1994 estimating that cleaning up the sites in need of work could cost $75 billion.[91] Among Fortune 500 companies, almost one-quarter reported that the cleanup costs for toxic waste sites on the National Priorities List cost them more than $10 million.[92] More serious still are the implications of Superfund for small businesses, many of which have been sent into bankruptcy by the associated liability.[93] Indeed, the EPA has estimated that 30 percent of all hazardous waste site owners will be forced to file for bankruptcy.[94]

The failure of courts to restrain EPA's aggressive interpretation of this statute has not only caused bankruptcies. It has also led to the unavailability of environmental insurance.[95] Ironically, EPA has acknowledged that the current limited availability of insurance for certain entities is based in part on the fact that "courts in key jurisdictions have imposed retroactive liabilities on insurers for pollution damages and cleanup costs that were never intended to be covered."[96] Had the old presumption been in force, these courts almost certainly would not have arrived at this result.

A hopeful sign that this era was over and that the strong presumption against retroactivity would reappear came in 1988. In *Bowen v. Georgetown University Hospital*,[97] the Supreme Court held that the

Department of Health and Human Services lacked the power to adopt retroactive rules. Stating that "retroactivity is not favored in the law," the Court concluded that, consequently, "congressional enactments and administrative rules will not be construed to have retroactive effect unless their language requires this result." But not until the next decade did the presumption begin its real revival.[98]

The Strong Presumption—Revived?

In 1990, in an influential concurring opinion in *Kaiser Aluminum & Chemical Corp. v. Bonjorno*, Scalia urged the Court to "reaffirm the clear rule of construction that has been applied, except for these last two decades of confusion, since the beginning of the Republic and indeed since the early days of common law: absent specific indication to the contrary, the operation of nonpenal legislation is prospective only."[99] In that case, the Court refused to apply retrospectively to the date of a judgment a subsequent statute governing the calculation of postjudgment interest. But the Court also expressly refused to "reconcile the two lines of precedent represented by *Bradley* and *Georgetown* because, under either view, where congressional intent is clear, it governs," and five justices thought that Congress had plainly not intended to give the statute retrospective effect.[100]

Four years later, the Court accepted Scalia's invitation. By an eight-to-one vote in *Landgraf v. USI Film Products*, the Court, over Justice Blackmun's dissent and with a majority opinion written by Justice Stevens, revived a strong presumption against retroactivity.[101] The Civil Rights Act of 1991 allowed for the recovery of compensatory and punitive damages. The 1991 Act also permitted a trial by jury when such damages are sought. In *Landgraf*, the Court held that Congress had not spoken clearly enough to warrant the application of these provisions to a case that was pending on appeal when the 1991 Act had been enacted.

In adopting the 1991 Civil Rights Act, Congress had agreed not to agree; as part of a political compromise, Congress had omitted an elaborate retroactivity provision that was part of an earlier, vetoed bill, leaving the courts to determine whether the 1991 Act applied retroactively.[102] The *Landgraf* Court acknowledged that "our precedents on retroactivity left doubts about what default rule would apply in the absence of congressional guidance, and suggested that some provisions might apply to cases arising before enactment while others might not."[103]

In *Landgraf*, the Court resolved those doubts against the retroactive application of statutes. Reciting some of the history discussed in this volume, the Court adopted the following test:

• Has "Congress expressly prescribed the statute's proper reach;" that is, does the statute *expressly state* that it will apply—or not apply—to conduct occurring before its enactment? If so, "there is no need to resort to judicial default rules."
• If not, "the court must determine whether the new statute would have retroactive effect, *i.e.*, whether it would impair rights a party possessed when he acted, increase a party's liability for past conduct, or impose new duties with respect to transactions already completed. If the statute would operate retroactively, our traditional presumption teaches that it does not govern absent clear congressional intent favoring such a result."[104]

The *Landgraf* Court focused in particular on the amendment's provisions increasing liability for a defendant's conduct prior to enactment:

> The extent of a party's liability, in the civil context as well as the criminal, is an important legal consequence that cannot be ignored. Neither in *Bradley [v. Richmond School Bd.*, 416 U.S. 696 (1974)] itself, nor in any case before or since in which Congress had not clearly spoken, have we read a statute substantially increasing the monetary liability of a private party to apply to conduct occurring before the statute's enactment.[105] [citations omitted]

The *Landgraf* Court did hold, however, that jurisdictional or procedural rules may apply retroactively without express congressional command because they regulate "secondary" and not "primary" activity.[106]

Although Scalia agreed, he wrote separately to object to the Court's willingness "to let that clear statement [mandating retroactive application] be supplied not by the text of the law in question, but by individual legislators who participated in the enactment of the law, and even legislators in an earlier Congress which tried and failed to enact a similar law."[107] This willingness to employ legislative history, Scalia wrote, "effectively converts the 'clear statement' rule into a 'discernible legislative intent' rule—and even that understates the difference."[108] Scalia also took the Court to task for not overruling *Thorpe* and *Bradley*, leaving the door open to future mischief.[109]

Since *Landgraf*, several appellate courts have applied its analysis in determining that a federal statute does not apply retroactively. For example, the Ninth Circuit recently rejected the retroactive application of a law extending civil forfeiture to funds that, while not involved in or traceable to a money-laundering enterprise, were in an account that previously contained money involved in such an illegal activity.[110] Similarly, the Sixth Circuit rejected retroactive application of provisions in the 1992 Television Consumer Protection Act that prohibited franchising authorities from granting exclusive franchises, on the grounds that the act "lacked 'strong and imperative language'" requiring retroactive application of this aspect of the act.[111]

In *Hughes Aircraft Company v. United States*,[112] which was decided at the end of the 1996–1997 term, a unanimous Supreme Court refused to apply retroactively amendments adopted in 1986 that allowed fraud suits on behalf of the government (known as *qui tam* actions), even if the information on which the *qui tam* action is based was known to the government. Before the amendments, *qui tam* suits could be based only on information of which the government was unaware. The Court therefore dismissed a suit based on allegedly false claims submitted in 1982 and 1984.

The Court rejected the argument that Justice Story's "'influential definition' of impermissibly retroactive legislation," which had been quoted with approval in *Landgraf*, "define[s] the outer limit of impermissible retroactivity." The Court continued:

> Rather, our opinion in Landgraf, like that of Justice Story, merely described that any such effect constituted a sufficient, rather than a necessary, condition for invoking the principle against retroactivity. Indeed we recognized that the Court has used various formulations to describe the "functional conceptio[n] of 'legislative retroactivity,'" and made no suggestion that Justice Story's formulation was the exclusive definition of presumptively impermissible retroactive legislation.[113]

The good news is that the Court in *Hughes* has broadened the category of laws that it will consider to be retroactive. The unfortunate news is that it has still not articulated fully a standard for assessing whether a law is "retroactive."

Thus, the rule today appears to have tacked back in the direction of the days before the Warren Court: "If the statute would operate retroactively, our traditional presumption teaches that it does not govern absent clear congressional intent favoring such a result."[114]

Picking up on Scalia's concurrence in *Landgraf*, Lund notes that the current antiretroactivity rule still is not as forceful as it might be. The Court apparently would allow the presumption against the retroactive application of statutes to be "overcome by ordinary techniques of statutory interpretation (such as evidence from legislative history or the applications of canons like *expressio unius*)."[115] Under this approach, Lund continues, the presumption "runs the risk of becoming just one of several factors that courts can manipulate virtually at will."[116] He prefers Scalia's clear-statement approach, which would require the text of the statute to declare plainly that it is to be applied retroactively.[117]

In sum, today we live in a world where Congress can legislate retroactively, so long as a court finds an intention to do so. The *Landgraf* presumption therefore does provide some protection against the inadvertent adoption of retroactive legislation. It also guards against the application of laws retroactively where Congress has not directly addressed the issue, or done so ambiguously. But Congress still needs not embody in the text of its legislation a clear statement that it intends a law to be applied retroactively. And, as discussed in the next part, today there are few constitutional impediments to the retroactive application of a civil law where Congress has clearly stated its intention that the law be so applied.

Part Two

---❖---

CONSTITUTIONAL CONSTRAINTS ON RETROACTIVE CIVIL LEGISLATION

4

THE EX POST FACTO
CLAUSES

Article I, section 9 of the Constitution provides: "No Bill of Attainder or ex post facto Law shall be passed." As currently interpreted, this provision prevents Congress from passing legislative determinations of punishment or retroactive *criminal* laws. Freedom from ex post facto laws and bills of attainder were considered so important that they are the only two individual liberties that the original Constitution protects from both federal *and* state intrusion. Article I, section 10 of the Constitution provides: "No State shall . . . pass any . . . *ex post facto* Law."

Certainly there are no more famous constitutional provisions prohibiting retroactive legislation than the ex post facto clauses. Indeed, many people mistakenly equate ex post facto laws with retroactive legislation, and they assume that the two are simply different ways of saying the same thing. They are not; especially as currently understood, ex post facto laws are a subset of the broader class of retroactive legislation.

Most important, based on its 1798 decision in *Calder v. Bull*, the Supreme Court has taken the position that the ex post facto clauses bar the adoption of retrospective *criminal* laws only.[1] Thus, it might seem to the reader that the ex post facto clauses are of little relevance to this study, which primarily focuses on retroactive *civil* legislation. A brief recitation of the debate about the scope of the clauses, however, illustrates that the case for a bar on retroactive civil legislation may be closer than many constitutional lawyers commonly believe. This observation further suggests the need to avoid such legislation, to the extent possible.

The Constitutional Convention

According to the great (and iconoclastic) constitutional scholar William Crosskey, when the Constitutional Convention met in 1789,

> the country had just been through a period when the making of *'ex post facto* laws' had been greatly abused in many of the states. The extreme dishonesty of some of their laws, like the so-called 'pine-barren' law of South Carolina, or the paper money acts of Rhode Island, had disgusted many men.[2]

On August 22, 1787, Elbridge Gerry and James McHenry moved to insert the following language: "The Legislature shall pass no Bill of Attainder nor any *ex post facto* law."[3] Gerry argued that this prohibition was more necessary with respect to the federal government than to the states, because there were fewer federal legislators. Thus, the federal legislature was, presumably, easier to corrupt. Gouverneur Morris opposed the motion, believing "the precaution as to *ex post facto* clauses unnecessary; but essential as to bills of attainder."[4]

Oliver Ellsworth of Connecticut, echoing the natural rights tradition, "contended that there was no lawyer, no civilian who would not say that *ex post facto* laws were void of themselves. It cannot then be necessary to prohibit them," he argued.[5] James Wilson appears to have agreed.[6]

Seemingly arguing in favor of including the prohibition in the Constitution, Daniel Carroll of Maryland, according to Madison, "remarked that experience overruled all other calculations. It had proved that in whatever light they might be viewed by civilians or others, the State Legislatures had passed them, and they had taken effect."[7] Wilson countered, remarking that just as such restrictions on ex post facto laws in state constitutions had been ineffective, insertion of such a clause into the federal Constitution was "useless."[8]

Hugh Williamson then pointed to North Carolina's prohibition of ex post facto laws. He acknowledged that the prohibition had been violated, but argued that "it has done good there & may do good here, because the Judges can take hold of it."[9] Dr. William Samuel Johnson of Connecticut countered; he thought the clause unnecessary, and implying "improper suspicion of the National Legislature." The clause then passed, seven to three.[10]

There was apparently a question as to the scope and meaning of this prohibition on ex post facto laws; one week later, James Dickinson reported that, on examining Blackstone's *Commentaries*, he found that "the terms *'ex post facto'* related to criminal cases only; that they would not consequently restrain the States from retrospective laws in civil cases, and that some further provision for this purpose would be requisite."[11] (As shall be seen, this reading of Blackstone is not without controversy.[12])

More than two weeks later, on Friday, September 14, 1787, after the Committee of Style had reported the ex post facto clauses in their current form, Colonel George Mason of Virginia moved to strike the prohibition against ex post facto laws. Madison reports that Mason "thought it not sufficiently clear that the prohibition meant by this phrase was limited to cases of a criminal nature—and no Legislature ever did or can altogether avoid them in Civil cases."[13] Gerry sought to clarify this ambiguity by having the prohibition apply to "Civil cases." Gerry's view was unanimously rejected. The next day, Mason sought to summarize his objection to embodying in the Constitution a rule that he believed to be unenforceable. Mason said:

> Both the general legislature and the State legislature are expressly prohibited from making *ex post facto* laws; though there never was nor can be a legislature but must and will make such laws, when necessity and the public safety require them; which will hereafter be a breach of all of the Constitutions in the Union, and afford precedent for other innovations.[14]

Thus, when the Convention ended, it was clear that neither the states nor the federal government could pass an ex post facto law. The scope of that prohibition remained to be seen.

Calder v. Bull

The Court addressed the issue of scope in one of its earliest constitutional decisions. The facts of *Calder v. Bull* have been briefly described above.[15] Without dissent, the Court held that the Connecticut legislature's setting aside of a judicial decree, and order of a new trial in a will contest, was not an ex post facto law forbidden under Article I, section 10. Justice Chase contended that the words ex post facto law "were technical, they had been in use long before the revolution, and had acquired an appropriate meaning, by legislators, lawyers, and authors."[16] Looking to Blackstone, state constitutions, and *The Federalist Papers*, Chase concluded that ex post facto laws were those that retroactively "create or aggravate the crime; or increase the punishment, or change the rules of evidence, for the purpose of conviction."[17]

Chase also made the compelling point that, had the ex post facto clauses barred all retroactive civil laws, the prohibitions on the impairment of contracts by states and on uncompensated takings by the federal government would have been unnecessary. This remains the best argument in favor of the Court's ultimate conclusion. Paterson agreed with Chase for many of the same reasons,[18] while Iredell agreed for reasons of policy.[19]

Although *Calder* seemingly held that the ex post facto clause applied to criminal legislation only, some believed that this question had not been squarely presented in *Calder v. Bull*. Connecticut did not have a written constitution at the time the dispute arose. Thus it was arguable that the Connecticut legislature, which also served a judicial function, was undertaking a judicial act in reviving the claim of Bull and his wife. One Supreme Court justice later argued that because the Connecticut legislature possessed a "controlling and revising power over the controversy," the question of "whether the phrase *ex post facto* was confined to criminal law" could not "arise in this cause."[20]

Thus, ten years after that decision, there was still some controversy about whether the Supreme Court was irrevocably committed to the proposition that the ex post facto clause was limited to criminal laws only.[21] But in 1854, when the Supreme Court upheld a retrospective change in estate tax law, it treated *Calder v. Bull* as establishing precisely that proposition.[22] The Court stated that "the debates in the federal convention upon the constitution show that the terms *ex post facto* laws were understood in a restricted sense, relating to criminal cases only, and that the description of Blackstone of such laws was referred to for their meaning."[23]

Critiques of *Calder v. Bull*

Since *Calder* was decided, many learned individuals have contended that the ex post facto clause indeed applies to civil legislation as well.[24] This view was expressed most strongly in 1829 by Justice William Johnson. He attached an appendix to the case of *Satterlee v. Matthewson*, which he asked to be included at the end of the volume reporting that case.[25] Johnson's "Note on the Exposition of the Phrase, '*ex post facto*,' in the Constitution of the United States" takes strong issue with the conclusion in *Calder v. Bull* that ex post facto laws refer to criminal prohibitions only.[26]

Johnson's critique of *Calder* took two forms. First, he contended that *Calder v. Bull* did not properly present the question whether the ex post facto clauses applied to civil legislation. Thus, he argued, the *Calder* Court's statements on the issue were unnecessary, and should be ignored.

Second, Johnson contended that "the phrase *ex post facto* is not confined, in its ordinary signification, to criminal law, or criminal statutes."[27] In support of this position, Johnson contended, among other things, that:

• The English case of *Wilkinson v. Meyer*, 2 Ld. Raym. 1350-52, used the phrase ex post facto to describe a civil law to require the registration of certain contracts, thus establishing that the phrase "had not received a practical or technical construction, which confined it to criminal cases."[28]

• Blackstone was misunderstood; he was commenting on the definition of an ex post facto law generally, and had used criminal laws as an example, but did not definitively declare that ex post facto laws were criminal only.[29]

• The comment in *Federalist* 44, on which *Calder* had relied, shed no light on the precise issue.[30]

• The constitutions of Massachusetts and Delaware, which the Court had cited in *Calder v. Bull* as confining the application of the phrase ex post facto to criminal cases, do not even contain the phrase.[31]

• The other two state constitutions cited in *Calder*, those of Maryland and North Carolina, would have applied the phrase generally, and in any event should not control the inquiry.[32]

In setting forth all this, and more, Johnson makes a strong case. But he has difficulty explaining why the contracts clause was necessary if the ex post facto clauses apply to civil and criminal statutes alike. Here he slips into a policy argument that suggests the strength of this point against him. Says Johnson: "The learned judges could not have foreseen the great variety of forms in which the violations of private right have since been presented to this court."[33] In fact, Johnson never provides a satisfactory explanation of why the contracts clause would have been necessary under his theory.

Two commentators have attempted to turn this point around,

however. In a recent and lengthy article on the subject of retroactive civil legislation, Laura Ricciardi and Michael Sinclair, supporters of Justice Johnson's conclusion, argue that because the bill of attainder clauses apply to criminal laws as well, under the Chase-Paterson argument in *Calder*, that provision is similarly redundant because it would clearly be encompassed within the meaning of an ex post facto law.[34] If we are entitled to presume that the ex post facto and contracts clauses have different meanings, they maintain, "then by parity [this argument form] must also be an adequate demonstration that they cannot be criminal laws either. Retrospective criminal laws had already been covered by the prohibition on bills of attainder."[35] They conclude that the ex post facto clause bars retrospective laws, such as tax laws, that are not covered either by the bill of attainder clause or the contracts clause.

Crosskey emphatically agreed that the ex post facto clause barred civil and criminal laws.[36] He points to fascinating evidence of contemporary newspapers suggesting that "*ex post facto* laws and retrospective laws are synonymous terms."[37] Crosskey, as is his wont, is not much troubled by the point on which Johnson falters. Crosskey argues that the purpose of the contracts clause is to divest the states of all power over contract law, and to vest it entirely in the federal government.[38] Although consistent with the rest of his argument—that the commerce clause denies the states any power over commerce—this view has not been accepted by any courts or by the vast majority of scholars.

There is one other point that Justice Johnson failed to expressly make, although he alluded to it: the problem with defining a clause in the Constitution according to its "technical meaning" according to "legislators, lawyers, and authors," and not as it is understood by "civilians."[39] This difficult question pitting intentionalists against those who subscribe to a jurisprudence of original understanding need not be resolved here.[40] Indeed, the conflict may not even exist. As one commentator early in this century concluded, on the basis of the records of the Constitutional Convention, the framers "did not give evidence of using the term *ex post facto* in a technical sense. The tendency seemed to be to impart a civil meaning to the term; there is no evidence of the term being used in different connections."[41]

These arguments have force but are ultimately unpersuasive. Even as currently construed, the ex post facto and the bill of attainder clauses are not redundant. Congress could pass a prospective law requiring an identifiable individual to be punished in the future, without making reference to past actions. Such a law would be a bill of attainder, but would not necessarily be an ex post facto law. Also, reading the ex post facto clause as applying to civil laws would prohibit any law transferring property from A to B. Such an interpretation would make the takings clause redundant.

Ricciardi and Sinclair also place too much weight on the maxim of construction that documents should be construed to avoid redundancy. The Constitution does contain overlapping provisions, both of which could apply in a given situation. For example, a soldier who moves into one's home without consent could well invade rights under the Third and Fourth Amendments to be safe from quartering soldiers and to be secure in one's house against unreasonable searches and seizures. Thus the arguments of Ricciardi and Sinclair are not quite forceful enough to upset two hundred years of settled practice. The evidence that the ex post facto clauses bar retrospective civil *and* criminal laws, although stronger than many have supposed, is not sufficiently clear to warrant urging (or expecting) the Supreme Court to overrule *Calder v. Bull*.

Distinguishing Civil from Criminal Laws

Although the Supreme Court has hewn to the position that the ex post facto clauses prohibit criminal penalties only, the Court has also, appropriately, applied the clause in civil cases where the civil disabilities are disguised as criminal penalties.[42] As the Court has said, "it is the effect, not the form, of the law that determines whether it is *ex post facto*."[43]

When undertaking this inquiry, courts assess whether the ostensibly civil fine or penalty is penal in nature.[44] "In determining whether legislation that bases a disqualification on the occurring of a certain past event imposes a punishment, the Court has sought to discern the objects on which the enactment in question was focused."[45] As Justice Frankfurter articulated the inquiry:

> The mark of an *ex post facto* law is the imposition of what can fairly be designated punishment for past acts. The question in each case where unpleasant consequences are brought to bear upon an individual for prior conduct, is whether the legislative aim was to punish that individual for past activity, or whether the restriction of the individual comes about as a relevant incident to a regulation of a present situation, such as the proper qualifications for a profession.[46]

This is clearly an appropriate examination; the legislature should not be able to avoid the Constitution's prohibition on ex post facto laws merely by characterizing as civil a retroactive penalty that is criminal in substance. But the Court has faltered in this analysis, in large part because of doctrinal developments concerning other clauses of the Constitution.

Most notably, the same question of what constitutes a "punishment" is relevant under the Fifth Amendment's double jeopardy clause, which provides: "Nor shall any person be subject to the same offense to be twice put in jeopardy of life or limb."[47] Although Justices Scalia and Thomas believe that this clause prohibits successive prosecutions only and not successive punishments,[48] the double jeopardy clause is generally interpreted as prohibiting the government from punishing a person twice for the same offense.[49]

Recent interpretations of the double jeopardy clause raise troubling implications for the ex post facto clauses.[50] Seeking to limit the force of the double jeopardy clause, the Court has adopted a very narrow view of what constitutes punishment. For example, in *United States v. Halper*,[51] the Supreme Court said that if "civil proceedings . . . advance punitive as well as remedial goals," they do not constitute punishment that is prohibited under the double jeopardy clause—nor, presumably, under the ex post facto clauses. In *Halper*, where the Court did invalidate a fixed civil penalty as violative of double jeopardy, the Court said:

> We have recognized in other contexts that punishment serves the twin aims of retribution and deterrence. . . . [I]t follows that a civil sanction cannot fairly be said solely to serve a remedial purpose, but rather can only be explained as also serving either retributive or deterrent purposes, is punishment, as we have come to understand the term. . . . We therefore hold that under the Double Jeopardy Clause a defendant who already has been punished in a criminal prosecution may not be subjected to an additional civil sanction to the extent that the second sanction may not be fairly characterized as remedial, but only as a deterrent or retribution.[52]

Applying this analysis at the end of the 1996 judicial term, however, the Court held in *United States v. Ursery* that the double jeopardy clause was not violated by a postconviction civil forfeiture action brought directly against the property ("in rem") based on the same underlying facts that gave rise to a criminal prosecution.[53] The Court found that confiscating the home of an individual convicted for growing marijuana was a "civil remedial sanction" and not a civil penalty. Justice Stevens dissented, attacking the "notorious fiction" that "the property, not the owner, is being 'punished' for offenses of which it is 'guilty.'"[54] Relying "on common sense," he concluded that "there is simply no rational basis for characterizing the seizure of this respondent's home as anything other than punishment for his crime."[55]

Under this analysis of "punishment," it therefore appears that, to be barred by the ex post facto clauses, a retroactive civil sanction will fail only if the sanction "may not be fairly characterized as remedial, but *only* as a deterrent or retribution."[56] Whatever the merits of such a limited view of punishment in the double jeopardy context—and, to be sure, it would be odd to have different analyses of the same concept for the ex post facto and the double jeopardy clauses—this approach considerably narrows the scope of the ex post facto clauses.

The Court's limited view of what constitutes punishment therefore suggests that the ex post facto clauses might not, for example, impede a legislature's *post hoc* confiscation of property, as long as the government had articulated some remedial justification for the confiscation. Although it may be that the takings clause would then be implicated by such a hypothetical circumstance, the Court's (apparently unintentional) narrowing of the ex post facto clauses is cause for concern.[57] Rather than a long discussion of how the Supreme Court has approached civil forfeitures, which was featured in *United States v. Ursery*, one longs for a careful analysis of whether, as an original matter, such a forfeiture would have been considered punitive. This dilemma highlights the general problem with the Court's current interpretation of the ex post facto clauses: the fact that many criminal laws can be rephrased as civil.[58]

As currently understood, the ex post facto clauses thus guard against only the most severe use of the legislature's power to make laws retroactive. They do so effectively where personal liberty is at issue. But the clauses are of little use to those who are aggrieved by most forms of retroactive civil legislation, which frequently affect property rights of one form or another.

5

❖

THE BILL OF
ATTAINDER CLAUSES

Coupled with the Constitution's proscription of ex post facto laws is a similar prohibition against bills of attainder being passed by Congress or the states.[1] Professor Raoul Berger argues with force that the bill of attainder clause protects against legislative actions that affect the *life* of the individual; according to Berger, it was not intended to encompass "bills of pains and penalties" that affected property rights.[2] (Presumably, the takings clause was intended to protect against federal confiscation of property without compensation.)

Even as expanded, however, the bill of attainder clause provides only limited protection against retroactive civil legislation. The modern Court rarely invokes the clause's protection; it has not invalidated legislation on a bill of attainder grounds since 1965. Moreover, the only laws that the Court has invalidated as bills of attainder have been bars on the employment of specific individuals or groups of individuals.

The Original Understanding of Bills of Attainder

At common law, bills of attainder were legislative acts that, without trial, condemned specifically designated persons or groups to death. Bills of attainder also required the "corruption of blood"; that is, they denied to the condemned's heirs the right to inherit his estate. Bills of pains and penalties, in contrast, singled out designated persons or groups for punishment less than death—such as banishment or disenfranchisement.

Parliament regularly passed both types of bills in times of rebellion and political turmoil, so that the Crown could easily purge those accused of treason. A famous 1685 attainder, which helped give rise to the Glorious Revolution of 1688, illustrates the point:

> Whereas James, Duke of Monmouth, has in an hostile manner invaded this kingdom and is now in open rebellion, levying war against the king, contrary to the duty of his allegiance; Be by and with the advice and consent of the lords spiritual and temporal, and commons in this parliament assemble, and by the authority of the same, That the said James Duke of Monmouth stand and be convicted and attainted of high treason, and that he suffer pains of death, and incur all forfeitures as a traitor convicted and attainted of high treason.[3]

Although Parliament used both types of bills to punish traitors, it carefully distinguished between true bills of attainder, imposing death, and the less severe bills of pains and penalties.[4] Likewise, colonial statutes regarding such bills (often aimed at Tories) observed this distinction. New York's Constitution, for example, distinguished between bills of attainder and legislative disenfranchisement when outlawing the two.[5] Other colonies routinely passed legislation calling for banishment or confiscation of property; all considered such laws to be bills of pains and penalties and not bills of attainder. Thus, when the framers barred bills of attainder, they presumably meant bills of attainder, and not bills of pains and penalties.[6]

Early Supreme Court Applications of the Clauses

Early Supreme Court decisions, however, interpreted the bill of attainder clauses as barring both bills of attainder and bills of pains and penalties. As early as 1810, for example, the Court conflated the two by stating that "a Bill of Attainder may affect the life of an individual, or may confiscate his property, or may do both."[7] By 1866, the Court had explicitly enlarged the Constitution's proscription of bills of attainder. Although acknowledging that acts inflicting punishments less than death were technically bills of pains and penalties, the Court held that "within the meaning of the Constitution, bills of attainder include bills of pains and penalties."[8] The Constitution, the Court thought, did more than merely ban traditional bills of attainder. Instead, the

Constitution sought broadly to prevent the legislature from "exercis[ing] the power and office of judge" to punish specific parties by depriving them of life, liberty, property, or political or civil rights.[9]

The Court thus used the bill of attainder clause to invalidate a Missouri law excluding from employment persons who refused to swear under oath that they had not aided or sympathized with the Confederacy,[10] and a federal act barring from the practice of law persons who had not also so sworn.[11] The Court reasoned that the oaths were not designed to gauge one's professional qualifications, but rather to punish those who associated with the Confederacy. Moreover, the oaths punished specific, identifiable persons defined by irreversible acts that they had committed. The bill of attainder clause, the Court concluded, precluded singling out such groups for this type of deprivation.[12]

The Court's Current View of the Bill of Attainder Clauses

The Warren Court expanded the bill of attainder clause even further, reading into it a broad separation-of-powers protection against trial by legislature.[13] The Court specifically rejected a "narrow historical approach" to the clause, and recharacterized the framers' purpose as not merely to bar true bills of attainder but to prohibit "legislative punishment, of any form or severity, of specifically designated persons or groups."[14]

Applying this test, the Court invalidated a statute making it a crime for anyone who was, or within the past five years had been, a member of the Communist party to hold a union office.[15] Because of the law's specificity, the Court reasoned that the act did more than preclude from positions affecting interstate commerce those whose past subversive conduct suggested that they might engage in political strikes. Instead, the prohibited law worked a legislative, not judicial, determination that members of the Communist party would, by their very nature, engage in illegal subversive conduct. This conclusion, coupled with preclusion from union office, constituted punishment within the Court's view of the clause's meaning.[16]

The Court has refused to broaden further the scope of the clause's protection. It continues to define a bill of attainder as a "law that legislatively determines guilt and inflicts punishment upon an identifiable individual without provision of the protections of a judicial trial."[17] Despite this rather broad formulation, the Court has devised tests to determine when a piece of legislation meets these three requirements— specification of the affected persons, punishment, and lack of a judicial trial.[18] Applying these principles, the Court rarely, if ever, invalidates legislation on this basis. This reluctance stems largely from the Court's narrow definition of punishment, discussed above.[19] Aside from historical practices such as banishment, disenfranchisement, and confiscation of property, only statutes that prohibit chosen individuals or groups from certain professions have been held to constitute modern bills of attainder. For example, the Court has held that the denial of noncontractual government benefits such as financial aid was not punishment,[20] nor did an act requisitioning the recordings and materials of President Nixon and several of his aides constitute punishment.[21]

In sum, although the Court may be reading the Constitution's prohibition on bills of attainder more broadly than the clause's history supports, even this expanded reading provides little protection against retroactive civil legislation. The Court's narrow definition of punishment enables legislatures to impose a wide variety of retroactive burdens before running afoul of the bill of attainder clauses.

6

THE CONTRACTS
CLAUSE

The contracts clause provides: "No State shall . . . pass any . . . Law Impairing the Obligation of Contracts."[1] At least two important points need to be made about this clause at the outset. First, the contracts clause restrains the states only, perhaps because, as Professor Michael McConnell has suggested, its primary purpose was to preserve interstate commerce. The contracts clause also may constrain the states only because, as smaller units of government, they are more susceptible to what Madison called "factious combinations" that could form a tyrannical majority.[2] Second, a raging debate exists about whether the contracts clause was intended to apply prospectively, as well as retrospectively. Because this volume focuses on retroactive legislation only, that vexing question need not detain us.[3]

Professors Douglas Kmiec and John McGinnis define the contracts clause as follows: "Correctly interpreted, the contracts clause prohibits all retrospective, redistributive legislation which violates vested contractual rights by transferring all or part of the benefit of a bargain from one contracting party to another."[4] They adduce three bases for this interpretation: first, the history of the clause supports it; second, this construction can be neutrally applied; and third, this construction comports with the framers' ideal of government—"namely a government constrained by a concept of the rule of law, restrained in circumstances which present particular risks of majoritarian disregard for minority rights, and rendered stable by barriers against abrupt change in social policy and organization."[5] They also correctly note that the Supreme Court no longer applies the plain meaning of the contracts clause.

The Origins of the Contracts Clause

The contracts clause was adopted against a background of widespread state abrogation of contracts, particularly in the form of debtor relief.[6] On August 28, 1787, Rufus King moved to add a provision from the Northwest Ordinance, which Congress had passed just six weeks earlier, prohibiting the states from interfering with private contracts. The ordinance provided that "in the just preservation of rights and property, it is understood and declared, that no law ought ever to be made, or have force in the said territory, that shall in any manner whatever interfere with, or affect private contracts, or engagements, bona fide, and without fraud previously formed."[7]

Gouverneur Morris objected, claiming that,

> this would be going too far. There are a thousand laws relating to bringing actions—limitations of actions & which affect contracts—The Judicial power of the U— S— will be a protection in cases within their jurisdiction; and within the State itself a majority must rule, whatever may be the mischief done among themselves.[8]

Madison acknowledged that "inconveniences might arise from such a prohibition but thought on the whole it would be overbalanced by the utility of it."[9]

Mason agreed with Morris. He made the same objection that he had made to the prohibition against ex post facto laws—that "[c]ases will happen that can not be foreseen, where some kind of interference will be proper, & essential." James Wilson countered, answering that "*retrospective* interferences only are to be prohibited."[10] Madison asked whether that was not "already done by the prohibition of *ex post facto* laws."[11]

A substitute motion was then made that would forbid states from passing "bills of Attainder or retrospective laws." That motion passed. Later on, John Dickinson reported (perhaps mistakenly, as noted above) that, according to Blackstone, ex post facto laws applied to criminal legislation only.[12] Two weeks after that, the clause was changed so as to bar states from "impairing the obligation of contracts."[13] Gerry suggested that the contracts clause be applied to the federal government as well. His motion was not seconded.[14] (This history, incidentally, further supports the Supreme Court's view, expressed in *Calder v. Bull*, that the ex post facto clause does not apply to civil legislation.)

The Contracts Clause in the Supreme Court

The Supreme Court's approach to the contracts clause can be divided into four separate periods. The first is the period from the founding until approximately the 1880s. During this time, the Court was faithful to the original understanding of the clause. In fact, the Court may even have applied the clause too broadly. The second period began after the Civil War and lasted through the 1930s. During this time, the contracts clause was largely treated as unnecessary because of the aggressive application of the doctrine of substantive due process. Next is the period during which the contracts clause fell into disrepute, along with substantive due process. The fourth period is the past two decades, when the Court has revived a weak version of the contracts clause.

The Early Period. As Kmiec and McGinnis report, "[F]or the first eighty years, the contracts clause appears to have generated more Supreme Court cases than any other constitutional provision—reflecting the original importance of the clause."[15] The first major case was *Fletcher v. Peck*,[16] mentioned above, in which the Marshall Court invalidated an attempt by the Georgia legislature to revoke a land grant. This decision was significant in that it applied the contracts clause to public as well as private contracts, broadly construed the term "contract," and amounted to a near absolute prohibition on impairments of contracts.[17]

Other significant Marshall Court decisions include *Sturges v. Crowninshield*,[18] which struck down a New York bankruptcy law that discharged a debt owing in contract, and *Dartmouth College v. Woodward*,[19] which invalidated New Hampshire legislation changing the college's charter and expanding the governor's power over the college.[20] The Court may not always have been correct in its application of the contracts clause during this period.[21] But the key point is that, until the post–Civil War period, the contracts clause was applied in a manner generally faithful to its original understanding: it was interpreted to affect more than debtor-relief legislation and to bar all retroactive alterations of contracts. "Moreover," according to Kmiec and McGinnis, "the Court correctly rejected the argument that the state's compelling interest in advancing the welfare of some group—in modern terms the state's use of its police power to advance the public welfare—justified contractual impairments."[22]

The Post–Civil War Period. The period during and after the Civil War witnessed a dramatic expansion in the power and role of government generally, and of the national government particularly.[23] Many commentators identify the beginning of the clause's decline with the 1879 decision of *Stone v. Mississippi*,[24] where the Court permitted a state to amend a corporate charter to forbid the corporation from selling lobbying tickets, even though the charter had initially granted the corporation such a right. There is a fair point to be made that the state was, in *Stone*, acting in its regulatory and not its proprietary capacity, and that *Dartmouth College* had construed the contracts clause too broadly by applying it to corporate charters.[25] Nonetheless, it is undeniable that, in recognizing a police power exception to the clause, *Stone* paved the way for the ultimate evisceration of the clause in the 1930s.

After *Stone*, the Supreme Court began using the doctrine of economic substantive due process to analyze, and generally strike down, laws that might properly have been assessed under the contracts clause.[26] As Rappaport notes, "during the *Lochner* era, the Court viewed both the contracts clause and the due process clause as involving the balancing of economic rights with the public interest."[27] Kmiec and McGinnis nicely summarize what occurred: "Misinterpreted as a form of substantive economic due process, the [Contracts] Clause was wrongly discredited when that doctrine was rightly discarded."[28]

The Contracts Clause Eviscerated. Under attack throughout the first part of the twentieth century and especially during the 1930s for impeding attempts at progress, the Supreme Court presaged the aforementioned 1937 "switch in time that saved nine" in its 1934 decision in *Home Loan Building & Loan Association v. Blaisdell*.[29] In *Blaisdell*, the Court upheld debtor-relief legislation that was precisely the type of law that the contracts clause was meant to prohibit. The Court explicitly rejected the original understanding of the clause, holding instead that the Court must consider the case "in light of our whole experience and not merely in that of what was said a hundred years ago."[30] The Court therefore upheld the legislation on the grounds that it: was emergency legislation; protected society and not particular individuals; imposed reasonable conditions; and was temporary in operation.[31]

Later that year, and during 1935 and 1936, the Court did find that the contracts clause prohibited three state statutes that impaired contracts in particularly egregious ways. For example, in *W.B. Worthen Co. v. Thomas*,[32] the Court invalidated an Arkansas law that exempted the proceeds of a life insurance policy from collection by the beneficiary's judgment creditors. The Court also struck down an Arkansas law that diluted the rights and remedies of mortgage holders,[33] as well as a law that modified the existing withdrawal rights of a building and loan association.[34]

But after the "switch in time," the contracts clause essentially fell into disuse.[35] In fact, so intermeshed had the contracts clause and due process clause become by 1960, that one commentator addressing the issue of retroactivity felt comfortable ignoring the contracts clause. He accurately commented that "no Supreme Court decision in the last 25 years dealing with contracts has been found that did not contain language to the effect that what was said about the contracts clause was equally applicable to the claimant's charge that he was being deprived of property without due process of law."[36]

Current Contracts Clause Jurisprudence. In the late 1970s, the Court began analyzing, and in some cases even invalidating, state legislation under the contracts clause. In *United States Trust v. New Jersey*,[37] the Court struck down state legislation that had retroactively repealed limits upon the Port Authority's ability to subsidize passenger transportation from revenues pledged as security for Port Authority bonds. The Court adopted a balancing test that asked whether the impairment was "reasonable and necessary to serve an important public purpose."[38] In addition, the Court required states, especially where their self-interest was apparent, to show that they had imposed the least restrictive impairment.[39] The next year, the Court struck down Minnesota legislation ordering corporations with pension plans to pay benefits to employees whose benefits had not yet vested under the contract between the employer and the employee.[40]

Although these cases suggest a revival of a moderate version of the contracts clause, Kmiec and McGinnis have noted that:

> The revival of the [contracts] clause . . . falls far short of restoring it to the power it should enjoy, given the original intention of the Framers. Moreover, the present Court's jurisprudence is at odds with the Framers' interest in providing certainty to those who enter into contracts, because in evaluating the constitutionality of an impairment the Court has

adopted widely different standards of review and balanced the extent of the impairment against the policy that the state seeks to advance. Based on an ad hoc policy calculus, the Court's decisions are largely unpredictable.[41]

The Court's failure to enforce the contracts clause according to its original understanding has dramatically weakened the substantive restraints on the ability of state legislatures to adopt retroactive civil laws. The early Court barred state legislation that mandated "any deviation from [a contract's terms], by postponing or accelerating the period of performance which it prescribes, impos[es] conditions not expressed in the contract, or dispens[es] with the performance of those which are, however minute, or apparently immaterial, in their effect upon the contract of the parties."[42] It is doubtful that the Court will soon restore that rule. Thus, retroactive civil legislation can most likely be limited only by the development of a political consensus, and procedural mechanisms, against such legislation.

7

THE FIFTH AMENDMENT'S PROHIBITION AGAINST UNCOMPENSATED TAKINGS

In addition to the imposition of criminal liability for an act that was lawful at the time it was committed, giving the property of A to B is often discussed as the paradigm of retroactive legislation.[1] Such legislation unquestionably upsets investment-backed expectations of the most firm variety. By prohibiting uncompensated takings, the framers explicitly banned such legislation where just compensation was not provided.

The takings clause of the Constitution states: "nor shall private property be taken for public use without just compensation." (It is worth noting that twenty-six states have constitutional provisions that require compensation for private property "damaged"—as opposed to confiscated—by state action. These provisions are therefore stronger than the takings clause.) Originally, this clause constrained the federal government only. As Michael McConnell suggests, the framers evidently believed that it was up to a state and its citizens to determine the degree of protection that property rights were to be afforded.[2] Today, of course, the takings clause applies to the states, having been "incorporated" into the due process clause of the Fourteenth Amendment.[3] Despite this expansion of the clause's application, it has been interpreted so as to be relatively ineffective in protecting against the many infringements of property rights that are the hallmark of the regulatory state.

The Origins of the Takings Clause

The prohibition against uncompensated takings has its origin in the Magna Carta, adopted on fear of death by King John at Runnymede in 1215. Chapter 28 of that document provided: "No constable or other bailiff of ours shall take corn or other provisions from anyone without immediately tendering money therefore, unless he can have postponement thereof by permission of the seller."[4] These rights were extended to all British subjects in 1335.[5]

From that time forward, English common law strongly protected property. The major influence on the framers' view of private property was John Locke, who was himself mightily swayed by the English common law tradition.[6] Locke denied that external things were held in common by mankind; rather, Locke "awarded ownership of any *unowned* thing to its first possessor." Locke's theory was based on the notion that each person owned his or her own talent and labor: "Though the earth and all inferior creatures be common to all men, yet every man has a property in his own person; this nobody has any right to but himself. The labour of his body and the work of his hands we may say are properly his."[7] According to Locke, by an overwhelming margin, most of the value of the mixture of labor and property was ascribable to labor. Thus, "it being by [man] removed from the common state nature hath placed it in, it hath by this labour something annexed to it, that excludes the common right of other men."[8]

The Lockean view of property was dominant by the time that the Constitution was ratified.[9] Blackstone's *Commentaries* adopted Locke's theory of the state, and protection of property was a "central and recurrent feature of the political thought of the day."[10] A few examples suffice to prove this point. For example, William Penn stated in 1675 that it was a fundamental maxim of law that subjects have "an ownership, and undisturbed possession: that what they have is rightly theirs, and no body's else."[11]

Echoing Penn, the declaration of rights affixed to the Pennsylvania Constitution stated: "No part of a man's property can be justly taken from him, or applied to public uses, without his own consent, or that of his legal representatives." Years later, Gouverneur Morris observed during the debates over the Constitution that protection of property was the predominant reason for organized society:

> An accurate view of the matter would nevertheless prove that property was the main object of Society. The savage State was more favorable to liberty than the Civilized and sufficiently so to life. It was preferred by all men who had not acquired a taste for property; it was only renounced for the sake of property which would only be secured by the restraints of regular government.[12]

The framers had a broad conception of what property meant as well. For example, Madison described "property" as:

> that dominion which one man claims and exercises over the external things of the world, in exclusion of every other individual. In its larger and juster meaning, it embraces everything to which a man may attach a value and have a right; and which leaves to every one else the like advantage. In the former sense, a man's land, or merchandise, or money, is called his property. In the latter sense, a man has a property in his opinions and the free communication of them. He has a property of peculiar value in his religious opinions, and in the profession and practice dictated by them. He has a property very dear to him in the safety and liberty of his person. He has an equal property in the free use of his faculties, and free choice of the objects on which to employ them. In a word, as a man is said to have a right to his property, he may equally be said to have a property in his rights.[13]

The Constitution itself contains more than twenty provisions that either directly or indirectly protect property and economic rights. The framers crafted the system of checks and balances partly to protect property rights from the institution that they considered the greatest threat to property (and liberty)—the legislature. As the *Federalist Papers* say:

> Experience has proved a tendency in our governments to throw all power into the Legislative vortex. The Executives of the States are in general little more than Cyphers, the legislatures omnipotent. If no effectual check be devised for restraining the instability & encroachments of the latter, a revolution of some kind or other would be inevitable.[14]

Yet the power to take property via eminent domain for the public good was an accepted power of the sovereign. The takings clause balanced the two conflicting interests of private property and public accommodation by allowing takings for public use if just compensation was paid.

The Takings Clause in the Supreme Court

Despite its seemingly all-embracing terminology, the takings clause was initially interpreted to constrain the federal government only.[15] In 1848, the Court again showed that the federal Constitution provided no protection against state government takings. In *West River Bridge v. Dix*, the Court concluded that "private rights vested under the government . . . are by necessary implication, held in subordination to [the eminent domain] power, and must yield in every instance to its proper exercise."[16] During the nineteenth century, the Court did establish the principle that the takings clause applied to takings of many kinds of property. Intangible property, such as patents and copyrights, was found to be protected by the takings clause.[17]

States had analogous provisions in their constitutions. As many scholars have noted, state courts often saw the Fifth Amendment as an embodiment of a universally applicable "higher" law, and applied it in takings cases even absent a specific state constitutional provision.[18] During the nineteenth century, state courts developed many of the concepts that still shape takings decisions: (1) that takings must be for "public use"; (2) that compensation equal in value to the taken property was required for the "taking" to be constitutional; (3) that procedural unfairness, or a denial of due process, could defeat a taking of property. Yet many states failed to honor the requirements of compensation or public use. As one commentator notes: "The burden of actual practice was in stunning contrast to theory."[19]

So long as Congress's Article I powers, or the state legislatures' police powers, were constrained within traditional limits, a ban on prototypical "takings"—the condemnation or physical invasion of a person's real property for a public use, such as a right-of-way or a reservoir—was sufficient to guard against most exercises of governmental power trenching on property rights.[20] But, as noted above, the power of government expanded dramatically after the Civil War. And the Supreme Court, as Mr. Dooley famously said, was never far behind the "iliction returns." In 1887, in *Mugler v. Kansas*,[21] the Court upheld a local liquor prohibition as a valid exercise of a state's police power. In so doing, the Court suggested that a regulatory measure cannot constitute a taking. This statement was arguably unnecessary to the decision; at the time, the prohibition against uncompensated takings in the Fifth Amendment had not been applied to the states. But *Mugler* is still regarded as good law—and is often cited for the proposition that government may prohibit "noxious" uses of property, that is, uses of property akin to "public nuisances"—without having to pay compensation.

With the dramatic rise of the regulatory state, the threats to property interests expanded exponentially. In 1922, in *Pennsylvania Coal Co. v. Mahon*,[22] Justice Holmes reacted to this threat by suggesting that the takings clause applied beyond direct governmental appropriation of private property and beyond governmental action that was the functional equivalent of ouster. His opinion gave rise to another class of takings cases, now known as regulatory takings.[23] According to Sidak and Spulber, a regulatory taking occurs where "the owner of private property is not forced to sell it to the government pursuant to a condemnation action, but rather is allowed to keep his property subject to significant constraints concerning its use issued in the name of the state's police power."[24]

In *Pennsylvania Coal*, the Court found that a state law, the Kohler Act, had the same effect as a taking, and therefore required compensation. The Kohler Act forced the owners of coal mines, which had contracted with surface owners to mine the coal under their property, to preserve sufficient material beneath the surface to prevent subsidence. According to the Supreme Court, this law made it "commercially impracticable to mine certain coal" on one's property, which had "very nearly the same effect for constitutional purposes as appropriating it or destroying it."[25] Holmes wrote: "The general rule at least is, that while property may be regulated to a certain extent, if regulation goes too far it will be recognized as a taking."[26]

The Takings Clause Today

In the seventy-odd years of regulatory takings jurisprudence since *Mahon*, the Court has, in its own words, "generally eschewed any set formula for determining how far is too far, preferring to engage in essentially ad hoc, factual inquiries."[27] This point is exemplified in *Penn Central Transportation Co. v. New York City*.[28] In that case, the Court affirmed the New York Land Preservation Commission's right to prevent the Penn Central Transportation company from selling the air rights above Grand Central terminal to developers, who planned to build a skyscraper. In so doing, the Court said:

In engaging in these essentially ad hoc, factual inquiries, the Court's decisions have identified several factors that have particular significance. The economic impact of the regulation on the claimant and, particularly, the extent to which the regulation has interfered with distinct investment backed expectations, are of course, relevant considerations. So too is the character of the governmental action. A "taking" may more readily be found when the interference with property can be characterized as a physical invasion by government . . . , than when interference arises from some public program adjusting the benefits and burdens of economic life to promote the common good.[29]

Thus, the scope and effect of the protection against regulatory takings are to this date uncertain, although many learned commentators offer insightful suggestions on how to apply it.[30] There are, however, two categories of takings that are considered compensable "without case-specific inquiry into the public interest advanced in support of the restraint."[31] First are physical invasions, no matter how minute.[32] The second category, according to the Supreme Court, involves legislation "where regulation denies all economically beneficial or productive use of land."[33] Thus, although the takings clause protects against some of the most onerous examples of retroactive legislation and is evidently making somewhat of a comeback, as currently interpreted, it does not yet offer adequate protection against the many infringements on property that the regulatory state grinds out.

Contractual Commitments

A recent landmark decision points out an additional constraint on the ability of Congress to adopt retroactive legislation, at least without adequately compensating those whose rights are compromised by it. *United States v. Winstar Corp.*[34] involved a challenge to a most egregious example of retroactive legislation. When a large number of "thrifts," or savings and loan associations, failed in the 1980s during the savings and loan crisis, regulators sought to minimize the government's insurance exposure by encouraging healthy thrifts and outside investors to take over the ailing institutions in a series of supervisory mergers. To avoid pushing these healthy thrifts into default, the government promised that these acquisitions would be subject to a particular accounting treatment that would let them meet the reserve capital requirements imposed by federal regulations.

Congress then enacted the Financial Institutions Reform, Recovery and Enforcement Act of 1989 (FIRREA).[35] FIRREA changed the capitalization requirements, thus revoking the promises made to the acquiring thrifts, many of which failed as a direct result of the government's changed regime.

By a 7–2 vote, the Supreme Court rejected the government's argument that it could not be held to a promise to refrain from exercising its regulatory authority in the future unless that promise was unmistakably clear in the contract. The Court also rebuffed the contention that, as a sovereign act, the government's alteration of the capital reserve requirement could not trigger contractual liability. Instead, the Court held that the government could not surrender its sovereign power to regulate the thrift industry, but it could be held liable in damages for the contracts that were accordingly breached.

Winstar properly recognizes that if the government is to exercise the sovereign power to adopt retroactive legislation, it may have to make whole those who are disproportionately harmed by the legislature's action. *Winstar* thus illustrates an appropriate approach to retroactive legislation.

8

❖

SEPARATION OF POWERS
AND DUE PROCESS

There is a powerful temptation, to which some justices and commentators have succumbed, to declare retroactive legislation either beyond the power of the legislature or a per se violation of due process. Neither history nor current jurisprudence supports either of these notions.

Separation of Powers

The long tradition of retroactive legislation, and the Constitution's (as well as the Supreme Court's) recognition that some retroactive legislation is permissible, make it impossible to accept the argument that a retroactive imposition of liability is not a valid "law," as Justice Chase argued in *Calder v. Bull.*[1] However tempting it may be to assert that the legislature simply lacks the power to adopt most forms of retroactive legislation, such an argument would be, in some senses, a further extension of the natural law argument about the limits of legislative sovereignty that the Supreme Court appears to have rejected and which appears to be essentially undefinable.[2]

There are instances of retroactive legislation that would offend the separation of powers, however. These generally are laws that would interfere with the judiciary's power under Article III to say what the law is and to adjudicate particular cases and controversies.[3] The most famous example is *United States v. Klein*.[4] In that case, the Supreme Court refused to give effect to a statute that was said to "prescribe rules of decision to the Judicial Department of the government in cases pending before it."[5] Specifically, the Court invalidated an act of Congress that was passed while the case was on appeal, declaring that a presidential pardon was proof that an owner of property had aided in the rebellion, and therefore his property was forfeited. This enactment sought to change an earlier determination by the Supreme Court that possession of such a pardon was sufficient proof that an owner had *not* given aid to the rebellion, and thus was entitled to get his property back.

Read broadly, *Klein* is utterly inconsistent with *Thorpe* and *Bradley*, discussed above, and would seem to have been overruled by them. But *Klein* has not been read that broadly. It is not considered to apply when Congress "amend[s] applicable law."[6] *Klein* continues to forbid retroactive changes that are narrowly directed to particular cases or sets of cases.

Recently, in *Plaut v. Spendthrift Farms*,[7] the Supreme Court relied on separation-of-powers principles to strike down retroactive legislation purporting to "prescribe what the law was at an earlier time, when the act whose effect is controlled by the legislature occurred."[8] *Plaut* involved a statute commanding the federal courts to reinstate cases that had been dismissed on statute of limitations grounds. In invalidating this statute, Justice Scalia, writing for the majority, reviewed the constitutional history that gave rise to the separation of the judicial from the legislative power, most notably the tendency of state legislatures from 1780 to 1787 to "correct" judicial judgments.[9] One key purpose of Article III, Scalia demonstrated, was to guard against the legislative annulment of final judgments.

According to Justice Scalia, the Constitution prohibits retroactive legislation that "requires its own application in a case already finally adjudicated";[10] such legislation "does no more and no less than reverse a determination once made, in a particular case."[11] Thus, cases that have been finally adjudicated may not be affected by the legislature, and there are (somewhat fuzzy) limits on the legislature's ability to prescribe the rules of decision in particular pending cases. Other than these relatively extreme cases—which would perhaps be unconstitutional under other theories as well—the separation of powers doctrine does not effectively bar most forms of retroactive civil legislation.

The Requirement of Due Process

The constitutional provisions discussed above—that is, the ex post facto, bill of attainder, contracts, and takings clauses—are the only ones that may be invoked against laws that are unambiguously retroactive. The concept of due process is raised in two contexts as a defense against retroactive legislation. The more difficult challenge is to find support for the proposition that the due process clauses are offended by legislation that is unambiguously retroactive. But where legislation is not clear, if the presumption of prospectivity is not applied to ensure prospective application, then a party may be able at least to claim that retroactive application of an ambiguous statutory provision would violate due process.

The due process clauses of the Fifth and Fourteenth Amendments prohibit the federal and state governments, respectively, from depriving any person "of life, liberty, and property" without due process of law. As is well known, courts often apply the due process clause to require that a person be accorded the appropriate process; they have also found the clauses to have a substantive component. To many, this is oxymoronic; as John Hart Ely quipped, "'Substantive due process' is a contradiction in terms—sort of like saying 'green pastel redness.'"[12]

That said, as alluded to above, in the nineteenth century, courts regarded retroactive legislation that compromised vested rights as violating due process. This was not, however, the modern version of substantive due process, which assesses the "reasonableness" of the statute. Rather, some courts struck down retroactive legislation as, by definition, failing to provide adequate notice, and thus the "process" that was "due." Neither the strength of the government's interest nor the scope of the regulation was relevant.

Over time, this due process argument against retroactive laws became incorporated into the modern concept of substantive due process, which is more of a balancing test than a bright-line rule. As noted, this broader version swallowed up the contracts clause as well. When economic substantive due process was rejected, the fallout hurt the contracts clause, as well as the hostility to retroactive laws generally.

Thus, the due process clauses do not bar unambiguously retroactive legislation. First, the due process clause was arguably not originally intended to constrain the legislature at all, but merely required the courts to follow the applicable, governing law. Second, today's courts do not employ the doctrine of substantive due process against retroactive civil legislation. Third, although an argument can be made that retroactive legislation denies an individual procedural due process because the affected party has, by definition, been given neither notice nor an opportunity to be heard, any retroactive civil legislation that would be cognizable under the due process clause today might well violate the takings or contracts clauses as well.

The Origins of the Due Process Clause. The language of the due process clause comes from English common law. The first articulation is found in the Magna Carta. Chapter 39 provides that no freeman "shall be arrested, or detained in prison, or deprived of his freehold, or outlawed, or banished, or in any way molested . . . unless by the lawful judgment of his peers and by the law of the land." Chapter 3 of 28 Edw. III (1355) states: "No man of what state or condition he be, shall be put out of his lands or tenements nor taken, nor disinherited, nor put to death, without he be brought to answer by due process of law."

The original interpretation of due process limited the legislature's power to compromise procedures guaranteed the accused. It also required judges to follow the law, not to rule arbitrarily, and to follow the forms and procedures of the law of the land.[13] For example, the Delaware Declaration of Rights and Fundamental Rules provided

> that every Freeman for every Injury done him in his Goods, Lands or Person, by any other Person, ought to have Remedy by the Course of the Law of the Land, and ought to have Justice and Right for the Injury done to him freely without Sale, fully without any Denial, and speedily without Delay, according to the Law of the Land.[14]

Although the "law of the land" and "due process" may not appear to be the same concept, Alexander Hamilton observed that the Fifth Amendment clarified that the guarantee that no man shall be deprived of any right but by the law of the land had become "due process." Noted Hamilton, "The words 'due process' have a precise technical import, and are only applicable to the process and proceedings of the courts of justice; they can never be referred to an act of the legislature."[15]

Due Process in the Supreme Court. Through the middle of the nineteenth century, the Supreme Court spoke explicitly of the degree to which retroactive laws offended "natural justice."[16] The Court did not employ the rubric of "substantive due process," but the Court had implicitly accepted the vested rights reading of the due process clause, according to which the legislature could not transfer property from A to B. The essence of this view was that because due process requires adjudication, and because legislation is not adjudication, any legislation that directly works a deprivation of property violates due process.

This hybrid of procedure and substance differs from the more modern notion of substantive due process: it is not a reasonableness requirement, but rather a blanket prohibition on A-to-B laws and an absolute protection of vested rights. Reasonable regulation pursuant to the police power, which the Court blessed in *Mugler*,[17] was permissible either because the rights regulated were not vested or because all property is implicitly subject to the police power. Action pursuant to such power is, on this view, not a deprivation.[18]

By the late 1880s, the Supreme Court began using the substantive component of the due process clause to implement many of its conceptions of natural justice.[19] One of the key aspects of natural justice that the Court implemented under substantive due process was to strike down as unconstitutional those legislative acts that violated "vested rights." Notes one commentator: "The elevation of the policy against retroactivity to a principle of the natural law paved the way for its assimilation into the due process clauses of federal and state constitutions where it remains with varying degrees of force today."[20]

For example, the Court held that the revocation of prior approval of plans showing that a railroad was entitled to certain land to be a violation of the due process clause.[21] A statute abrogating war risk insurance contracts was held unconstitutional as applied to outstanding policies.[22] Had these laws not been applied retroactively, they probably would not have been vulnerable under a due process challenge.

Once the Court "switched" in 1937, however, it stopped applying substantive due process to invalidate economic legislation. A recent student commentator reports that "since the origination of the tax deference doctrine in 1938 [in *Welch v. Henry*[23]], the Supreme Court not only has never sustained a due process challenge to the retroactive application of a tax law, but, more remarkably, has not sustained a due process challenge to any retroactive economic law."[24]

The Problem with Using Due Process to Invalidate Retroactive Laws. It is tempting to contend that the due process clauses bar the adoption of retroactive legislation that interferes with vested rights. The problem is that, outside the context of the takings and contracts clauses, no one has ever satisfactorily defined a "vested right." And, as noted above, the enveloping grasp of the due process clause has hurt legitimate assertions of the takings and contracts clauses.

As one commentator has observed:

> One's first impulse on undertaking to discuss retroactive laws and vested rights is to define a vested right. But when it appears, as soon happens, that this is impossible, one decides to fix the attention upon retroactive laws and leave the matter of definition to follow rather than proceed the discussion, assuming for the purpose that a right is vested when it is immune to destruction by retroactive legislation. The simplification of the task which this plan seems to involve turns out to be something of an illusion, however, when it appears, as also soon happens, that one's preconceived notion of retroactive laws are irreconcilable with the data with which one has to deal.[25]

The definition offered in the current *Black's Law Dictionary* illustrates the confusion about which rights are and are not "vested." *Black's* defines vested rights as:

> [R]ights which have so completely and definitely accrued to or settled in a person that they are not subject to be defeated or canceled by the act of any other private person, and which it is right and equitable that the government should recognize and protect, as being lawful in themselves, . . . Such interests as cannot be interfered with by retrospective laws . . . .[26]

In short, under this doctrine, retroactive laws that infringe on vested rights are unconstitutional, and vested rights are defined as those that cannot be interfered with by retroactive laws. The definitions are entirely circular.

Some have attempted to define what is and is not a vested right by looking at what rights courts have and have not protected. Thus, some examples of "vested rights" identified by courts include: perfected liens; the interest revested in the granter of a void deed; the recipient who has already been given a gift (for gift tax purposes); and an accrued but as yet unenforced cause of action at common law.[27] Examples of claims not held to be "vested rights" include: a mere expectancy, such as a water permit under which no water had been used; a particular remedy, so long as another adequate remedy exists; a particular jurisdictional or venue rule; a particular rule of evidence; a term of public office; legal grounds for divorce; the defense of contributory negligence; or the route of a public highway.[28] This is hardly a satisfactory approach, however. Past experience is instructive, but absent a principle; it does not tell us what rule of decision to apply in the future.

Does Retroactive Legislation Receive Enhanced Scrutiny Today? On occasion, the Court has said that retroactive legislation warrants greater scrutiny under the due process clauses. For example, the Court has remarked that, although the constitutionality of economic legislation is generally presumed, "it does not follow . . . that what Congress can legislate prospectively it can legislate retrospectively. The retrospective aspects of legislation, as well as the prospective aspects, must meet the test of due process, and the justifications for the latter may not suffice for the former."[29] But as Eule states, "the occasional noises emanating from the Court, designed to remind us that the [due process] route is not foreclosed, have a hollow ring to them."[30]

Perhaps the best example of the futility of asserting a due process challenge to retroactive legislation is the aforementioned case of *United States v. Carlton*.[31] There, the Court concluded that due process was not offended by Congress's passage of a retroactively applied law that altered the deductibility of a certain stock sale. The Court was unpersuaded by the taxpayer's argument that the retroactive statute violated due process because he detrimentally relied on it when he sold certain shares. Nor did the Court consider the taxpayer's contention that he was denied notice in violation of due process.

But at least some members of the Court recognized just how outrageous the result was. As Scalia remarked:

> If I thought that "substantive due process" were a constitutional right rather than an oxymoron, I would think it would be violated by bait and switch taxation. Although there is not much precision in the concept "harsh and oppressive," which is what this Court has adopted as its test in the field of retroactive tax legislation, surely it would cover a retroactive amendment that cost a taxpayer who relied on the original statute's clear meaning over $600,000.[32]

Thus, today the Court continues to pay some lip service to the notion that the constitutionality of retroactive legislation is, in Scalia's terms, "conditioned upon a rationality requirement beyond that applied to other legislation."[33] But the Court does not exercise this power to scrutinize retroactive legislation more strictly. Rather, the Court applies the lenient "rational basis" test to retroactive economic legislation, just as it does to prospective economic legislation.[34] As currently interpreted, the due process clause does not impede a legislature from adopting retroactive laws.

Void for Vagueness

Related to due process, and to the anti-retroactivity principle, is the notion that a statute can be void for vagueness because it is not sufficiently clear to give those affected by the rule adequate notice of the legislature's intention. This doctrine recognizes that where the legislature has not adequately specified the scope of its prohibition, it is unjust to punish an individual for violating such a prohibition. Vague laws, as the Supreme Court said in 1925, "leave open . . . the widest conceivable inquiry, the scope of which no one can foresee and the result of which no one can foreshadow or adequately guard against."[35]

This doctrine is, however, primarily applied in the criminal context, or in the service of express constitutional protections—most notably, the First Amendment. In fact, it appears only to have been applied in one civil case, during the height of the *Lochner* era. In *A.B. Small Co. v. American Sugar Refining Co.*,[36] the Court invalidated a statute that limited a seller to no more than a "reasonable profit." The Court said that "the exaction of obedience to the rule or standard . . . was so vague and indefinite as really to be no rule or standard at all."[37] This standard is not often met. Thus, the void-for-vagueness doctrine serves somewhat as a check on the unanticipated application of laws without adequate notice, but it has not served as a major impediment to retroactive civil legislation.

Vagueness and Due Process in the Administrative Context

Although courts have not invalidated unambiguously retroactive legislation on the grounds that those subject to it were not given sufficient notice to satisfy the due process clause, courts have limited the power of administrative agencies to enforce regulations that fail "to give fair warning of the conduct [they] prohibit or require."[38] More promising yet is that agencies have been denied the power to assess liability retroactively, even as the interpretation of the statute giving rise to that liability has been upheld as a "reasonable interpretation" within the agency's discretion. This important line of cases can serve as a check on the application of legislation in a retroactive manner.

Rollins Environmental Services v. EPA[39] exemplifies this line of cases. That case involved an EPA regulation requiring that any container holding PCBs, a toxic contaminant, "be decontaminated by flushing the internal surfaces of the container three times with a solvent containing less than 50 ppm PCB. . . . *The solvent may be used for decontamination until it contains 50 ppm PCB. The solvent shall then be disposed of as a PCB . . . .*"[40] After each rinse, Rollins analyzed the solvent to ensure that the PCB concentration was below 50 ppm PCB. The company then incinerated the solvent in a manner that did not comply with EPA's regulations under the Toxic Substance Control Act (TSCA) but that *did* comply with the Resource Conservation and Recovery Act (RCRA). As the court said, "Rollins followed this course because it believed, in light of the italicized portion [above], that *only* solvents having a PCB concentration of 50 ppm or more had to be disposed of as PCBs."[41]

Six years later, the EPA charged Rollins with violating TSCA, contending that "a particular PCB concentration cannot be avoided as a dilution."[42] The administrative law judge recognized that Rollins had reasonably interpreted the word "then" as referring to the point at which the solvent reaches a concentration of 50 or more ppm PCB and, consequently, as not requiring the disposal of the solvent as a PCB if it never reached that threshold. EPA, by contrast, read "then" to refer to the time when the rinsing is over and the solvent is no longer being reused. The court charitably described this interpretation as "rather more strained," and as one that "would not exactly leap out at even the most astute reader."[43]

The court nonetheless believed that it was obligated to sustain EPA's reading under the extremely deferential standards accorded an agency's interpretation of its own regulations.[44] But the court rejected the agency's finding that Rollins should be subjected to a $25,000 penalty and reinstated an earlier ALJ's determination that the appropriate penalty should be zero, because Rollins's "reading of the Regulations had a definite plausibility" and because "Rollins had proceeded with care, by burning the rinse in an incinerator approved under RCRA."[45] Specifically, the court said:

> When the agency itself is uncertain of the meaning of its regulation, when agency personnel give conflicting advice to private parties about how to interpret it, and when the agency's chief legal officer finds the regulatory language equally supportive of one of two possible constructions, it is impossible to find the regulation "clear." Ambiguity may be in the eyes of the beholder. But here EPA's imprecision, not Rollins' lack of acuity, led the company astray. No reasonable reader of

this provision could have known that EPA's current construction is what the agency must have had in mind.[46]

Concurring and dissenting in part, Judge Edwards would not even
have upheld the finding of liability (he agreed that the penalty should
be reduced to zero). The majority had found that Rollins's failure to
cite the due process clause meant that it had not preserved the argument that the regulation was unfairly applied to it. Edwards noted that
"[t]he whole point of petitioner's argument in this case had been that
a party cannot be found to have violated a regulatory provision absent
'fair warning' that the allegedly violative conduct was prohibited."[47]
Whether this is a constitutional issue—a question Edwards thought
the court did not need to reach—"it is a simple principle of administrative law that, in adopting administrative regulation, an agency 'has
the responsibility to state with ascertainable certainty what is meant by
the standards promulgated.'"[48]

Four years later, in a similar case, the D.C. Circuit unanimously
vacated a finding of liability and set aside a fine on the grounds that
the regulations did not provide the affected party with fair warning of
the agency's interpretation.[49] Relying in part on *Rollins*, Judge Tatel
referred to a long line of cases holding that "when the sanctions are
drastic . . . elementary fairness compels clarity in the statements and
regulations setting forth the actions to which the agency expects the
public to comply."[50]

Thus, even though courts do not often invoke vagueness or due
process concerns to invalidate unambiguous legislative determinations
that a statute should be applied retroactively, they are, apparently increasingly, willing to insist that agencies provide fair notice in the application of statutes to affected individuals. Given the size and scope
of the administrative state, this line of cases can serve as a powerful
check on the retroactive application of statutes, or regulations promulgated pursuant to statutes.

9

❖

THE CASE OF
SUPERFUND

At this point, it may be worth taking stock of the existing impediments to retroactive legislation and seeing whether, as properly or as currently understood, they effectively protect against the most notorious and egregious example of retroactive legislation countenanced during the *Thorpe-Bradley* era: Superfund. Superfund has already been discussed above to some extent.[1] The retroactive application of Superfund has also been the subject of at least two perspicacious articles by George Clemon Freeman,[2] and an eighty-plus page opinion, discussed below, in the case of *United States v. Olin*.[3] The purpose of the discussion here is not to document comprehensively CERCLA's many outrages but simply to apply the analysis discussed above.

Due in large part to the urging of the EPA and the acquiescence of the courts, Superfund retroactively imposes strict, joint, and several liability even on companies that disposed of wastes in a manner wholly in accordance with law. This means that liability lies without regard to fault. It also means that a party who may have contributed to 2 percent of the harm at a site may be forced to pay the entire cost of remediating the harm at that site. Anyone who contributed in any manner to waste at a particular site, even in a noncriminal or nonnegligent manner, is considered a "responsible party" by the EPA, and subject to liability under the Act. Even though the EPA may not in practice have pushed its power under CERCLA to the extreme, it continues to have the authority to do so.

Was CERCLA Meant to Be Applied Retroactively?

CERCLA's text certainly does not say that it should be applied retroactively. CERCLA's liability provision, section 107(a), does use the past tense, specifically covering those who "arranged for" disposal or treatment of wastes. But liability under this section turns on a "release" or "threatened release." Arranging for the disposition that leads to a release or threatened release is necessarily antecedent to such a release.[4] Thus, the use of the past tense cannot be dispositive of the retroactivity issue.

Moreover, although section 107(f) precludes recovery for damages to natural resources where such damages and the release happened wholly before CERCLA, this does not mean the rest of the act was meant to apply retroactively. In fact, this precise use of "negative implications" as a means of finding an intention to apply a statute retroactively was rejected in *Landgraf*.[5] Rather, section 107(f) merely suggests that section 107 and some other sections have some application to preenactment conduct.

Nor does the legislative history, which has been rehearsed at length by others, establish a clear intention to apply CERCLA retroactively. Congress acted on Superfund so hastily that no conference reports exist, and the committee reports are essentially useless.[6] As Freeman reports:

> On the specific issue of liability for pre-enactment conduct, there were two conflicting points of view not resolved one way or another in the language of Superfund. One point of view was that persons who arranged for disposal of hazardous wastes at an existing site should somehow be held responsible for any required cleanup. The contrasting view was concerned about the unfairness and potential unconstitutionality of any retroactive application, fearing that retroactive application would result in the collapse of insurance markets, with the attendant threat to United States businesses, large and small.[7]

The EPA has argued that Congress intended to force the cleanup of old dumpsites, and that "responsible" parties should be required to bear a proper share of the costs of the cleanup.[8] But CERCLA did not have to be interpreted as imposing retroactive, joint, and several liability to have meaning; it could easily have been construed as applying prospectively and as creating a new federal procedural remedy (as opposed to substantive liability) for preenactment conduct that was either illegal or actionable under preexisting state or federal law.[9]

In addition, applying CERCLA retroactively ignores the Superfund mechanism. Superfund is an approximately $8.5 billion fund generated by taxes on chemicals, oils, and corporations having taxable income in excess of $2 million.[10] The fund provides the means to clean up preenactment waste sites. Given this alternative reading, which would include provisions for past waste sites, applying CERCLA retroactively was unwarranted.

Courts and the Retroactivity of CERCLA

Neither the text nor the legislative history of CERCLA shows a clear intention to apply the statute retroactively. Had the strong *Landgraf* rule of prospectivity been in effect, the courts almost certainly would have applied CERCLA prospectively. Before *Landgraf*, however, a number of courts held that CERCLA liability does arise based on actions taken before CERCLA's enactment. A majority of these were district court decisions holding that the imposition of liability *was* retroactive—namely, that the language of CERCLA, or the legislative history, or both demonstrated that Congress intended CERCLA liability to be applied retroactively.[11] As noted above, many of them did so under the influence of *Thorpe* and *Bradley*. A minority of the courts, including a few federal courts of appeal, held that such liability was not technically retroactive, because the harm from the disposal continued after enactment.[12]

This latter argument is somewhat, but not much, harder to refute. Under the retroactivity analysis outlined at the outset of this volume, the appropriate focus should be on the affected behavior—that is, the actor's knowledge at the time it undertook the relevant action giving rise to the liability. A key question in assessing whether a law is impliedly retroactive is: what did the affected party know, and when did he know it? Many of the companies now being charged by the EPA under CERCLA did not know at the time that their activity caused harm and had no reason to expect that they were engaged in an unlawful activity. Moreover, some even obtained permits to engage in the very activities for which they are now being punished. Thus the application of CERCLA to them is clearly retroactive. The government may not punish past behavior by declaring the continuing effects of that behavior harmful, unlawful, or a nuisance.

United States v. Olin

In May of 1996, a federal district judge in Alabama, Senior Judge Brevard Hand, ruled that CERCLA does not apply to waste discharged before its 1980 effective date.[13] (The court also ruled that, as to waste discharged after 1980, CERCLA's application in this case violated the commerce clause—an issue that this volume does not address.) The court's extensive decision was rendered, essentially on the court's own motion, in the context of a dismissal of a consent decree entered into between the Olin Corporation and the Environmental Protection Agency concerning sites where "most of the alleged contamination resulting from the operation of these two plants occurred prior to the effective date of CERCLA, December 11, 1980."[14]

Taking a fresh look at the subject of retroactivity, the court in *Olin* determined that, in light of *Landgraf*, CERCLA liability should be applied prospectively. The court concluded that CERCLA's language did not dictate its retroactive application and that the sparse legislative history likewise contained no such clear intent. The court further noted that CERCLA's strict, joint, and several liability scheme is more Draconian than the compensatory relief under Title VII of the Civil Rights Act of 1964 that the Supreme Court refused to apply retroactively in *Landgraf*. The *Olin* court therefore found no clear indication that Congress intended CERCLA to apply retroactively and dismissed the consent decree to the extent that it held Olin responsible for waste discharged prior to enactment.

In so doing, the *Olin* court commented:

> [The Department of] Justice confuses what it, the EPA, and a number of courts consider desirable with what it can be said Congress clearly intended. Insofar as pre-enactment releases are concerned, the purpose of CERCLA can be covered through the Superfund. The EPA, however, has chosen to recover as much as possible from private parties, no doubt in part due to Congress' failure to provide sufficient resources to pay for cleaning all the sites, even as the need was thought to be in 1980 . . . . [L]ack of funding does not render the operation of the statute itself ineffective in the sense used in *Landgraf*. . . . Nothing presented in the Justice Department

brief or pre-*Landgraf* cases concerning the statutory language of CERCLA or its legislative history demonstrates that Section 107(a) is "the sort of provision that must be understood to operate retroactively because a contrary reading would render it ineffective.[15]

The court also rejected the roughly two dozen cases applying CERCLA retroactively because they had been decided before *Landgraf*.[16]

In light of *Landgraf*, it is perhaps surprising that some in the legal community were shocked by *Olin*'s holding that CERCLA's basic liability provision, CERCLA section 107(a), is inapplicable to waste deposited before the date of the statute's enactment.[17] Had *Landgraf* been decided a decade ago, the numerous intervening decisions upholding the retroactive application of CERCLA almost certainly would have been resolved differently. As George Freeman, whom the *Olin* court cited, stated:

> Had the *Landgraf* decision and its predecessor, *Bowen v. Georgetown University Hospital*, existed in the early 1980s, the host of cases that were misled by the broad dicta of *Bradley v. Richmond School Board* to hold Superfund retroactive would have been decided differently. . . . [I]f the question were before a federal court today in a case of first impression, Superfund's liability provision, section 107(a), could not meet the test of statutory construction set forth in Justice Stevens' majority opinion in *Landgraf*.[18]

Unfortunately, despite the soundness of the district court's application of *Landgraf*, the Eleventh Circuit Court of Appeals reversed the district judge's careful and extensive opinion in a fairly perfunctory analysis. The court acknowledged that "CERCLA contains no explicit statutory command regarding retroactive application of its cleanup liability."[19] Under *Landgraf*, this should have ended the analysis. Focusing on Congress's use of the past tense to impose liability on "any person who at the time of the disposal of any hazardous substance owned or operated the facility," the appellate court concluded that "Congress manifested a clear intent to reach conduct preceding CERCLA's enactment."[20] The Eleventh Circuit also relied on the legislative history to buttress its conclusion. Thus, the one vehicle that might have forced the Supreme Court to confront the question of CERCLA's retroactive application was squelched at the appellate level.

Is Retroactive Application of CERCLA Constitutional?

A number of constitutional arguments have been made against the retroactive application of CERCLA.[21] Despite CERCLA's evident unfairness, most of these arguments are unavailing, particularly under current case law. This conclusion highlights the importance of the presumption of prospectivity and the need for a political consensus and procedural mechanisms against retroactive legislation.

Some contend that Superfund is a prohibited ex post facto law and a bill of attainder. The first argument is not without force. This retroactive nature of the statute, combined with strict, joint, and several liability, allows an argument that the retroactive application of CERCLA is punitive. If punitive, of course, the ex post facto clause, which bars retroactive punishments, could be implicated.

Specifically, trying to prove the punitive nature of the statute, when it is applied retroactively, Freeman shows that the

full thrust of EPA's interpretation of Superfund is that an off-site generator of waste may be liable:

(i)   in huge amounts;
(ii)   on the basis of only the most marginal connection with the particular release or threatened release;
(iii)   even in the absence of ordinary causation in fact;
(iv)   without rights of contribution against others who as a practical matter may have been more involved; and
(v)   on the basis of conduct that was not negligent, abnormally dangerous, or illegal.[22]

There is a temptation to say that the retroactive application of a law such as CERCLA simply cannot be constitutional. Superfund has cost companies millions of dollars in cleanup costs, and in many cases it has sent companies into bankruptcy.[23] As noted, the Congressional Budget Office released a report in January 1994 that estimated that it could take $75 billion to clean up the sites in need of work.[24] Further, the legal costs are astronomical; as *Insight Magazine* stated, the only parties that have "cleaned up" have been the lawyers.[25] The U.S. General Accounting Office surveyed the cleanup cost and legal expenses of the Fortune 500 Industrial and Fortune 500 Service corporations and, in December 1994, reported that twenty-two of the companies surveyed reported that the cleanup costs for toxic waste sites on the National Priorities List cost them over $10 million.[26] Moreover, CERCLA affects not only large companies, for many small businesses have incurred extraordinary costs or have been driven into bankruptcy as well.[27]

Given the magnitude of the costs involved, the length of time that CERCLA covers, in some cases stretching as far back as the nineteenth century, and the open-ended nature of the liabilities, CERCLA is far more egregious than even the retroactive tax increases discussed above. In fact, the differences are so great that they may amount to a difference in kind.

The Constitution, however, especially as originally understood, does not prohibit everything that is unfair or even outrageous. Carefully assessed, the argument that CERCLA is unconstitutional is in tension, at least, with the Supreme Court's current interpretation of the ex post facto and bill of attainder clauses. It may also be at odds with the original understanding of those clauses.

A Bill of Attainder? The contention that CERCLA violates the bill of attainder clause may be dispensed with easily. Under the Supreme Court's current case law, the class of "responsible parties" is almost certainly not sufficiently small to warrant treatment as a bill of attainder.[28] The Court, which has not struck down a law under the bill of attainder clause in thirty years, is not likely to consider CERCLA a "legislative punishment . . . of specifically designated persons or groups."[29] Moreover, as we have seen, the bill of attainder clause was originally understood to prohibit laws that affected life and liberty only.[30]

An Ex Post Facto Law? Because the ex post facto clauses do not apply to civil laws, Superfund therefore would have to be characterized as punitive in nature to be classified as an ex post facto law. The current Court, though, has suggested that unless a law is exclusively punitive, it will not come within the scope of the ex post facto clauses. Although CERCLA certainly has a punitive element, it is hard to contend, under the relevant Supreme Court test, that it "may not be fairly characterized as remedial, but *only* as a deterrent or retribution."[31]

As an original matter, whether CERCLA is encompassed within the ex post facto clauses would depend on whether such a law would have been considered punitive by the common law at the time the Constitution was ratified. This is a difficult but important inquiry, although it is beyond the scope of this book. Freeman contends that "Superfund is analogous to earlier forms of governmental taking of all or part of a person's property because of past conduct," referring to bills of pains and penalties, as well as to amercements, which are similar to fines.[32]

This contention is certainly worth further study and is persuasive, although not necessarily dispositive. One difficulty with the argument is that, as noted, the framers deliberately prohibited "bills of attainder," not bills of pains and penalties. And, given the limitation of the ex post facto clauses to criminal laws, it remains to be seen if amercements were treated as criminally punitive at common law.

Substantive Due Process. Freeman's contention that CERCLA violates substantive due process does not require much discussion. Although the Court pays lip service to the notion that retroactive laws warrant more searching scrutiny than the rational basis test only, in practice the Court has stopped striking down economic legislation on substantive due process grounds.[33] As an original matter, of course, there is no such doctrine.

Takings. Whether the retroactive application of CERCLA is a taking remains a harder question, one that Freeman does not address. The current Court would probably not regard it as such, given the lack of a physical invasion and the ostensibly remedial purpose. As an original matter, CERCLA does not fit neatly into the takings box either. But one can contend that the government is taking money—which is certainly protected property[34]—for a "public purpose," that is, cleaning up property that the allegedly "responsible party" may not have been knowingly or negligently responsible for harming. This would particularly be true with respect to money spent to clean up pollution generated by others. In addition, CERCLA often requires the expenditure of funds in connection with a piece of property that far exceeds that property's value. This might well constitute a regulatory taking.

The key point, however, is that none of these arguments is without its difficulties, either under current Supreme Court precedent or as an original matter. Had the courts properly applied the presumption against retroactivity in first interpreting CERCLA, we would not need to explore the outer edges of the Constitution's protection against retroactive legislation.

10

❖

A SUGGESTION FOR
THE JUDICIARY AND A
POLITICAL SOLUTION

The Court should adopt the clear statement rule championed by Justice Scalia in his *Landgraf* concurrence. Recall that, under this view, a statute would be applied prospectively unless the text of that statute expressly declared that it was to be applied retroactively. A clear statement rule would be consistent with the rule of law, as well as with the proper institutional role of judges. It would constrain retroactive legislation without tying the legislature's hands. And it would assist courts in interpreting the legislature's intentions.

Although the Supreme Court has revived a strong presumption against retroactivity, it has still not adopted a clear statement rule that would require Congress to express, in text, a determination that a statute should apply retroactively. Moreover, as has been shown, in some cases the Constitution may not provide adequate protection against retroactive legislation. In still other cases, the Court has limited the constitutional constraints on Congress's power to adopt such statutes. Thus, in some areas, most notably taxation, retroactivity has become the rule rather than the exception.

A clear statement rule has obvious advantages:

• Such a rule would, according to Nelson Lund, "reduce the likelihood of inadvertently retroactive statutes, which can easily result when courts draw negative inferences from statutory language."[1]

• A clear statement rule would also, Lund notes, "prevent minority factions from unilaterally inserting retroactive features into statutes through interpretive comments in committee reports and floor statements."[2]

• A clear statement rule would promote accountability. Members of Congress would not be able to avoid the political implications of a retroactive law by claiming that the courts had misinterpreted their intentions.

• Clear statement rules are also a traditional way of avoiding close or hard constitutional issues.[3]

• A clear statement rule would, as one commentator notes, "restore judicial legitimacy by anchoring interpretation in a literalist reading of statutory terms. Decisions that are 'clearly compelled' by statutory language forestall the transformation of judicial interpretation into judicial legislation."[4]

• Most important, a clear statement rule would almost certainly dramatically reduce the instances of strong retroactivity because members of Congress would be reluctant to adopt such legislation, given the obvious fairness problems created by strongly retroactive legislation.

Urging the Court to adopt this approach may not be futile. The overwhelming majority of the Court did come close to adopting such a rule in *Landgraf*. And retroactive legislation is sufficiently antithetical to the American sense of fair play that a clear statement rule might attract even those justices who are less rule-oriented than Scalia.

The courts should also continue their revival of the takings clause. The advantage of the takings clause over any bar on retrospective legislation is that it still permits the government to undertake the desired retroactive action. Currently, retroactive action by the government is essentially "free." There is, accordingly, excess demand for such a technique; that is, retroactive legislation is too often employed.[5] If compensation for retroactivity were mandatory, it would be far more likely that the legislature would produce the optimal level of it.

The relevant test should be, as one recent court put it, whether a property owner can "demonstrate that [he] bought [his] property in reliance on a state of affairs that did not include the challenged regulatory regime."[6] As Sidak and Spulber point out, this "requirement is a means to impose a system of falsifiability of what could otherwise become an inherently subjective inquiry."[7] If an individual can objectively prove, through evidence of investment, that he detrimentally relied on the challenged regulatory regime, he should recover his lost property value.

The courts also should continue holding agencies to the requirement that they provide adequate notice before they enforce a statute or a regulation. In that respect, the line of authority represented by *Rollins v. EPA* is quite encouraging. There may be an argument that, as a matter of democratic theory, the legislature should have the power to change the rules in the middle of the game, so long as it does so clearly and after careful consideration. This argument becomes far more attenuated, however, when applied to agencies. Courts should prohibit agencies from depriving parties of property by imposing civil or criminal liability in the absence of clear notice.

A Political Solution

Laws that expressly refer to, and change, the past legal consequences of past events—the most easily identifiable types of retroactive laws—should be subject to a super-majority provision.[8] Impliedly retroactive and, of course, prospective laws present far more difficult problems.

To address these issues, Congress should adopt, and the president should sign, the provisions concerning retroactivity embodied in the Common Sense Legal Reforms Act of 1995. In addition to the super-majority requirement for all strongly and weakly retroactive laws, the bill would require Congress to have the committee originating any legislation, or perhaps the comptroller general, assess the effect of the proposed legislation on investment-backed expectations. This would address the issue of impliedly retroactive and prospective laws, that is, it would assess the retrospective effects of legislation that operates forward in time, but that may change the legal consequences of past events.

In conducting this inquiry, Congress should be guided by whether the past behavior that is affected by the legislation falls into the category of what Ricciardi and Sinclair call "nonreliance" behavior.[9] As they define it, nonreliance behavior is that behavior that a reasonable individual undertakes without "resort to the statute books" or other explicit reliance on the existing legal regime.[10] As Ricciardi and Sinclair put it, "[m]ost behavior is probably of this kind."

Any statute that proposes to regulate behavior that is, in Ricciardi and Sinclair's terms, "of the kind that people usually do not undertake without legal advice and planning,"[11] as determined by either the relevant congressional committee or the comptroller general, should be declared out of order. (Examples of such behavior include tax and estate planning, securities transactions, and most investments.) Any such statute should be subject to a point of order by a member of either House and put to an immediate vote. This mechanism would extend the recent congressional proposals, one of which was actually adopted by the House of Representatives, declaring out of order any proposal for a retroactive tax increase.

A third part of this bill should preclude agencies from enforcing statutes or regulations against individuals in the following circumstances: (1) where the regulation was so ambiguous that it did not provide fair notice; (2) where the individual reasonably relied on a written statement of agency policy that takes a different view; or (3) where the agency has not interpreted the statute or regulation, and the individual's reading of the statute or regulation is reasonable. A provision of this sort was included, in various forms, in many versions of the comprehensive regulatory reform package that was considered during the 104th Congress.[12] It is important not to go too far, and to permit individuals to rely on oral communications by agency personnel. Such a rule would discourage informal exchanges with agency personnel and raise many proof problems. But agencies should not be able to punish those who either reasonably rely on the agency's own statements or make good faith compliance efforts with which the agency ultimately disagrees.

In addition to the statute described above, the president should also adopt a retroactivity executive order. Modeled on the takings and federalism executive orders, such an order should require agencies and all executive branch officials to assess the implications of their proposed actions on investment-backed expectations. This is unlikely to make much of a difference, but it may help to bring some attention to, and raise consciousness about, the issue of retroactivity.

It is tempting to propose a constitutional amendment banning retroactive laws. A few reasons counsel against this course of action. First, constitutional amendments should be a mechanism of last, not first, resort. Other efforts should be made, along the lines proposed above, before we resort to a constitutional ban on retroactive legislation. Second, defining retroactivity is sufficiently difficult as to counsel against a constitutional amendment. Third, a constitutional ban on retroactive laws would give courts even more power than they have now vis-à-vis the legislature. In the United States today, the courts are

powerful enough. Fourth, there are a few occasions other than curative legislation where laws that could be characterized as retroactive
may be justified. To take one recent example, in 1994 Kansas enacted
a Sexually Violent Predator Act.[13] That act establishes procedures for
the civil commitment of persons who, due to a "mental abnormality"
or a "personality disorder," are likely to engage in "predatory acts of
sexual violence." The act was passed after one Leroy Hendricks committed his sexual crimes. Upon his release from prison, he was civilly
committed.[14]

Arguably, such a law is not retroactive, in that it requires an as-
sessment of an individual's present condition.[15] A court could, however, perhaps characterize the law as retroactive because the relevant
evidence relies on past behavior. (In fact, four justices characterized
the statute as an impermissible ex post facto law.[16]) A constitutional
amendment barring such laws, along with others that experience teaches
us to be justified, might therefore tip the balance too much in the
direction of stability. Thus, at least until the above-mentioned recom-
mendations have been tried, a constitutional amendment would not
be justified at this time.[17]

Every government decision maker has a duty to balance the com-
peting concerns of stability and flexibility; it is dangerous to rely too
much on the courts for protection against infringements on individual
liberty, much less for the preservation of settled, investment-backed
expectations. Procedural devices that facilitate such an inquiry can help
guard against unnecessary interference with the status quo while still
preserving the option of retrospectively readjusting benefits and burdens in the few circumstances where a sufficiently compelling case can
be made that such a remedy is necessary.

11

❖

CONCLUSION

Close cases must not obscure the clarity with which we understand the obnoxious nature of almost all retroactive legislation. Nor should we despair of ending most such legislation merely because the Constitution, especially as currently interpreted by the Supreme Court, does not invalidate these laws.

Rather than wait and hope for salvation by the courts, the best way to deal with the problem of legislation that unduly upsets expectations may be to build a political consensus against such laws. Retroactive laws in particular are so hostile to fundamental fairness that once their existence comes to light and they become a political issue, a consensus may form urging that they should be prohibited entirely, except where curative. At least as a first step in developing such a consensus, Congress should adopt procedures by which it enacts retroactive laws only if a clear consensus exists that they are necessary. It should adopt impliedly retroactive laws only after carefully considering whether to do so. In such cases, Congress's decision to alter the consequences of past events should be clearly embodied in the text of the statute.

Such a debate, which is analogous to the debate in the culture between the need for stability and the desirability of change, could have a beneficial spillover effect. Retroactive legislation strikes many people as unfair. Pointing to specific instances of expectations that have been unsettled by such legislation may be a more effective tactic in promoting stability than mere rhetoric. To some, change sounds progressive and good; but almost everyone relates to the unfairness of having the proverbial rug pulled out from under him.

One commentator has noted that

Retroactivity is always an aspect of the broader problem of weighing the interests in stability against the constant demands for change in the flux of modern life. Occasionally . . . retroactive legislation can be conscripted on the side of stability and there is little argument with its use for this purpose. The vestiges which survive of the early suspicion of retroactive legislation may reflect the attitude that if change is not urgent, the balance should be struck in favor of stability.[1]

There is no better reason to revive the aforementioned "early suspicion of retroactive legislation" than to rekindle the "attitude" that if change is not urgent, "the balance should be struck in favor of stability."

NOTES

CHAPTER 1: INTRODUCTION

1. LON L. FULLER, THE MORALITY OF LAW 53 (1964).

2. H. CLAY TRUMBULL, HINTS ON CHILD TRAINING 126 (1890).

3. *See* Michael J. Graetz, *Legal Transition: The Case of Retroactivity in Income Tax Revision*, 126 U. PA. L. REV. 47, 57–58 (1977).

4. Jill E. Fisch, *Retroactivity and Legal Change*, 110 HARV. L. REV. 1055, 1067 (1997) [hereinafter *Fisch*].

5. Douglas W. Kmiec & John O. McGinnis, *The Contract Clause: A Return to the Original Understanding*, 14 HASTINGS CONST. L. Q. 525, 528 (1987) [hereinafter *Kmiec & McGinnis*].

6. FULLER, *supra* note 1, at 60; Bryant Smith, *Retroactive Laws and Vested Rights*, 5 TEXAS L. REV. 231, 233 (1927) ("If . . . a law is retrospective which extinguishes rights acquired under previously existing laws, then all laws of any kind whatsoever, are retrospective. There is no such thing as a law that does not extinguish rights, powers, privileges, or immunities derived under existing law. That is what laws are for.") [hereinafter *Smith*].

7. W. David Slawson, *Constitutional and Legislative Considerations in Retroactive Lawmaking*, 48 CALIF. L. REV. 216, 226 (1960) [hereinafter *Slawson*].

8. U.S. Const. art. I, § 9.

9. *Id.*, § 10.

10. As one legal scholar has put it, "[E]volutionary theory (incorrectly) suggests that the law is always improving. Every change is self-proclaimed to be for the better." Herbert Hovenkamp, *Federalism Revised*, 34 HASTINGS L.J. 201, 215–16 (1982) (book review).

11. FULLER, *supra* note 1, at 59 (in analyzing retroactive legislation, "the most difficult problem of all [is] knowing when an enactment should properly be regarded as retrospective").

12. Julian N. Eule, *Temporal Limits on the Legislative Mandate: Entrenchment and Retroactivity*, 1987 AM. B. FOUND. RES. J. 379, 443 (1987).
13. *Id.*
14. 22 F.Cas. 756, 767 (C.C.D.N.H. 1814) (Story, J.).
15. *See infra* at 77–79.
16. Argument of Counsel in Poole v. Fleeger, 36 U.S. 185, 198 (1837) (*quoted
in Smith*, 5 TEX. L. REV. at 233–34 n.9); *see also infra* at 42.
17. *Smith*, 5 TEX. L. REV. at 232.
18. Stephen R. Munzer, *Retroactive Law*, 6 J. LEGAL STUD. 373, 383 (1977).
19. United States v. Carlton, 512 U.S. 26, 28 (1994).
20. 42 U.S.C. § 9601 *et seq.*
21. United States v. Monsanto Co., 858 F.2d 160, 167 (4th Cir. 1988), *cert.
denied*, 490 U.S. 1106 (1989).
22. David H. Topol, *Hazardous Waste and Bankruptcy: Confronting the
Unasked Questions*, 13 VA. ENVTL. L.J. 185, 190 (1994). *See generally* Richard
L. Stroup, *Superfund: The Shortcut That Failed* 6 (PERC Policy Series May
1995).
23. 83 Stat. 792, as amended by the Black Lung Benefits Act of 1972, 86
Stat. 150, 30 U.S.C. § 901 *et seq.*
24. *Slawson*, 48 CALIF. L. REV. at 238; *see* Laura Ricciardi & Michael B. W.
Sinclair, *Retroactive Civil Legislation*, 27 U. TOL. L. REV. 301, 345 (1996)
[hereinafter *Ricciardi & Sinclair*] (giving, as a modern example of a curative
law, Congress's enactment of the Portal-to-Portal Act of 1947, which had retroactive effect, and which changed a surprising judicial interpretation of a
statute, on which no one had relied).
25. This hypothetical is used by FULLER, *supra* note 1, at 53–54.
26. Some commentators have sought to define a technical distinction between retroactive and retrospective laws. Most do not. *See, e.g.*, Charles B.
Hochman, *The Supreme Court and the Constitutionality of Retroactive Legislation*, 73 HARV. L. REV. 692, 692 n.1 (1960) [hereinafter *Hochman*].
27. Bowen v. Georgetown University Hospital, 488 U.S. 204, 220 (1988)
(Scalia, J., concurring).
28. Landgraf v. USI Film Products, 511 U.S. 244, 281–86 (1994) (Scalia, J.,
concurring).
29. Nelson Lund, *Retroactivity, Institutional Incentives, and the Politics of
Civil Rights*, 1995 PUB. INTEREST L. REV. 87, 94 (1995) [hereinafter *Lund*].
30. *Bowen*, 488 U.S. at 220 ("A rule that has unreasonable secondary retroactivity—for example, altering future regulation in a manner that makes worth-
less substantial past investment incurred in reliance on the prior rule—may
for that reason be 'arbitrary' or 'capricious' . . . and thus invalid.") (Scalia, J.,
concurring).
31. *Fisch*, 110 HARV. L. REV. at 1103.
32. *Id.*
33. *Id.*
34. *Fisch*, 110 HARV. L. REV. at 1071.
35. *Hochman*, 73 HARV. L. REV. at 697.

36. For such a defense, *see* Antonin Scalia, *The Rule of Law as a Law of Rules*, 56 U. CHI. L. REV. 1175 (1989).

37. *Id.* at 1178.

38. *See, e.g.*, Jonathan R. Macey, *The Internal and External Costs and Benefits of* Stare Decisis, 65 CHI.-KENT. L. REV. 93, 98 (1989); *see generally* Daniel A. Farber & Philip P. Frickey, LAW AND PUBLIC CHOICE 7 (1991) (surveying the findings of public choice theory).

39. *See, e.g.*, *Retroactive Taxation Virtually Unlimited*, HOUSTON CHRON., June 14, 1994, § A at 5.

40. H.R. Res. 6, 104th Cong., 1st Sess., § 106(b) ("It shall not be in order to consider any bill, joint resolution, or conference report carrying a retroactive Federal income tax increase.").

41. S. 94, 104th Cong., 2d Sess. (approved by Governmental Affairs Committee, May 16, 1996).

42. H.R. 10, 104th Cong., 1st Sess. § 106(B).

43. U.S. Const. art. I (bicameralism, presentment, and enumerated powers of Congress); THE FEDERALIST NO., No. 51 (James Madison).

44. JOHN C. GRAY, NATURE AND SOURCES OF THE LAW 97 (1909) (*quoted in* Bryant Smith, *Retroactive Laws and Vested Rights*, 6 TEX. L. REV. at 409, 414 (1928).)

45. *Slawson*, 48 CALIF. L. REV. at 245 (1960) ("When presented with a set of facts the legal effect of which is disputed, a court has no choice but to give a decision.").

46. 1 W. BLACKSTONE, COMMENTARIES ON THE LAWS OF ENGLAND *70–72; Mishkin, *Foreword: The High Court, the Great Writ, and the Due Process of Time and Law*, 79 HARV. L. REV. 56, 58–60 (1965) (Blackstone's "declaratory theory" of common law proposes that a court apply its rules retroactively).

47. *Lund*, 1995 PUB. INTEREST L. REV. at 88 ("With the explosion of activism in the Warren Court era, the basic distinctions between judicial and legislative acts began to collapse").

48. *See, e.g.*, Linkletter v. Walker, 381 U.S. 618, 636 (1965) (applying the *Mapp* exclusionary rule prospectively).

49. *Fisch*, 110 HARV. L. REV. at 1070.

50. *See, e.g.*, Harper v. Virginia Dep't of Taxation, 509 U.S. 86 (1993).

51. *Id.* at 97.

52. *Id., quoting* Griffith v. Kentucky, 479 U.S. 314, 323 (1987).

53. The interested reader should consult William V. Luneberg, *Retroactivity and Administrative Rulemaking*, 1991 Duke L.J. 106 (1991) [hereinafter *Luneberg*]. Although I do not agree with most of Professor Luneberg's conclusions, the article provides helpful background.

54. *Bowen*, 488 U.S. 204 (1988).

55. It also bears mentioning that a presumption of retroactivity—i.e., a presumption opposite to the one examined here—applies to the repeal of punishments. As the Supreme Court said in 1809, "[I]t has been long settled, on general principles, that after the expiration or repeal of a law, no penalty can be enforced, nor punishment inflicted, for violations of the law committed

while it was in force, unless some special provision be made for that purpose by statute." Yeaton v. United States, 5 Cranch 281, 283 (1809). Accordingly, all of the legislation referred to here should be treated as if it is nonpenal; this qualification will not be reiterated each time the presumption against retroactive legislation is discussed.

56. 2 SINGER, SUTHERLAND STAT. CONST. § 41.03 n.9 (5th ed. 1984) (citing constitutional provisions). At least according to one commentator, "[i]n general, federal courts have offered significantly less opposition to retroactive legislation than state courts." Ray H. Greenblatt, *Judicial Limitations on Retroactive Civil Legislation*, 51 Nw. U. L. REV. 540, 543 (1956). An evaluation of the merits of this claim is beyond the scope of this article.

CHAPTER 2: MORAL AND ECONOMIC ARGUMENTS

1. *Romans* 5:15.
2. OLIVER WENDELL HOLMES, THE COMMON LAW 163 (43rd printing 1949).
3. BENJAMIN N. CARDOZO, THE GROWTH OF THE LAW 3 (1924).
4. JOHN LOCKE, SECOND TREATISE OF GOVERNMENT § 137, at 72 (1980).
5. Ronald A. Cass, *Judging: Norms and Incentives of Retrospective Decision-making*, 75 B.U. L. REV. 941, 954 (1995) [hereinafter *Cass*]; Charles B. Hochman, *The Supreme Court and the Constitutionality of Retroactive Legislation*, 73 HARV. L. REV. 692, 693 ("Perhaps the most fundamental reason why retroactive legislation is suspect stems from the principle that a person should be able to plan his conduct with reasonable certainty of the legal consequences.").
6. Grayned v. City of Rockford, 408 U.S. 104, 108 (1972) ("[B]ecause we assume that man is freed to steer between lawful and unlawful conduct, we insist that laws give the person of ordinary intelligence a reasonable opportunity to know what is prohibited so that he may act accordingly. . . .") (Marshall, J.).
7. W. David Slawson, *Constitutional and Legislative Considerations in Retroactive Lawmaking*, 48 CALIF. L. REV. 216, 224 (retroactive law "necessarily eliminates the possibility that its effects can be avoided by a choice of conduct") [hereinafter *Slawson*].
8. *See, e.g.*, United States v. Carlton 512 U.S. 26 (1994); United States v. Darusmont, 449 U.S. 292 (1981).
9. *Slawson*, 48 CALIF. L. REV. at 226 (discussing LON A. FULLER, PROBLEMS OF JURISPRUDENCE 701–03 (temp. ed. 1949)).
10. *Smith*, 6 TEX. L. REV. at 417.
11. *Id.*
12. FRIEDRICH A. HAYEK, THE CONSTITUTION OF LIBERTY 8, 29 (Phoenix ed., 1978).
13. Nelson Lund, *Retroactivity, Institutional Incentives, and the Politics of Civil Rights*, 1995 PUB. INTEREST L. REV. at 91.
14. *Slawson*, 48 CALIF. L. REV. at 245; *see also* City of Richmond v. J. A. Croson Co., 488 U.S. 469, 513–14 (1989) (Stevens, J., concurring) ("It is the judicial system, rather than the legislative process, that is best equipped to

identify past wrongdoers and to fashion remedies that will create the conditions that presumably would have existed had no wrong been committed.").

15. J. Gregory Sidak & Daniel F. Spulber, *Deregulatory Takings and Breach of the Regulatory Contract*, 71 N.Y.U. L. REV. 851, 865 (1996). [hereinafter *Sidak & Spulber*]

16. *Cass*, 75 B.U. L. REV. at 960.

17. *Id.* at 961 ("When decision-makers based their determinations on inaccurate value assessments, parties who cannot easily contract to reverse or modify such decisions are left with a result that is less valuable than an alternative outcome.")

18. J. GREGORY SIDAK & DANIEL F. SPULBER, DEREGULATORY TAKINGS AND THE REGULATORY CONTRACT: THE COMPETITIVE TRANSFORMATION NETWORK INDUSTRIES IN THE UNITED STATES 104–08 (1997).

19. *See, e.g.*, *ASEAN Officials to Draw up Framework for Regional Investment Area*, Deutsche Presse-Agentur, July 5, 1996 (describing investment area plan as protecting foreign assets from nationalization, to attract more foreign investment); *New Government in Bangladesh: Restoring Confidence*, EIU BUSINESS SOUTH ASIA, July 1, 1996 (noting that 1971 government "was responsible for ruining the new-born country's economy through nationalization of all industries. . . ."); Clyde Mitchell, *The Current Landscape in Egypt*, N.Y. L.J., March 20, 1996, at 3 ("Foreign investors responded [to strict regulation of ownership in 1958] by pulling out of Egypt . . . foreign investment participation in the economy drastically declined.").

20. Pablo T. Spiller, *Institutions and Regulatory Commitment in Utilities' Privatization*, 2 INDUS. CORP. CHANGE 387, 393 (1997).

21. *See, e.g.*, Michael J. Graetz, *Legal Transitions: The Case of Retroactivity in Income Tax Revision*, 126 U. PA. L. REV. 47, 49–63 (1977). [hereinafter *Graetz*]

22. *See, e.g., id.*

23. Louis Kaplow, *An Economic Analysis of Legal Transitions*, 99 HARV. L. REV. 511, 515–19.

24. Jill E. Fisch, *Retroactivity and Legal Change*, 110 HARV. L. REV. 1055, 1069 (1997).

25. *Fisch*, 110 HARV. L. REV. at 1088.

26. *Id.*

27. LON L. FULLER, THE MORALITY OF LAW 62 (1964).

28. Julian N. Eule, *Temporal Limits on the Legislative Mandate: Entrenchment and Retroactivity*, 1987 AM. B. FOUND. RES. J. 379, 439–40.

29. *Cass*, 75 B.U. L. REV., 950.

30. Daniel E. Troy, *Toy Story*, NEW REPUBLIC, June 12, 1996 (letter to the editor).

CHAPTER 3: RESURGENCE OF ANTIPATHY

1. Elmer E. Smead, *The Rule Against Retroactive Legislation: A Basic Principle of Jurisdiction*, 20 MINN. L. REV. 775, 775 (1936) (citing and quoting Corpus Juris Civilis, Code, 1, 14, 7) ("Leges et consuetutiones futuris certum

est dare formam negotii, non ad facta praeterita revocari, nisi nominatim etiam de praeterito tempore adhuc pendentibus negotiis cautum six." — Laws for the regulation of commerce should not revoke past agreements, unless those laws are necessary to provide certainty in business). [hereinafter *Smead*]

2. *Id.* at 776.

3. 2 Inst. 292, cited in *Smead*, 20 MINN. L. REV. at 777 n.7.

4. *Id.* at 777 n.8 (citing cases).

5. *Id.* at 780.

6. 1 BLACKSTONE, COMMENTARIES *46.

7. *Id.*

8. *Id.*

9. *Id.* (emphasis in original).

10. *Id.* (emphasis in original).

11. Dennis R. Nolan, *Sir William Blackstone and the New American Republic: A Study of Intellectual Impact*, 51 N.Y.U. L. REV. 731, 731–32 (1976) [hereinafter *Nolan*] ("Blackstone has been acclaimed as the prime influence on the Declaration of Independence, the United States Constitution, [and] the reception of the common law in America . . .) (footnotes and citations omitted).

12. FORREST MCDONALD, NOVUS ORDO SECLORUM: THE INTELLECTUAL ORIGINS OF THE CONSTITUTION XII (1985). As Dennis Nolan writes in a somewhat skeptical study of Blackstone's influence, of the subscribers to Bell's first American edition of Blackstone's COMMENTARIES, sixteen "became signatories of the Declaration of Independence, six were delegates to the 1787 Constitutional Convention, one was elected President of the United States and another became Chief Justice of the Supreme Court." *Nolan,* 51 N.Y.U. L. REV. at 743–44.

13. 3 U.S. (3 Dall.) 386 (1798).

14. *See* chapter 4.

15. *Calder*, 3 U.S. (3 Dall.) at 391.

16. DAVID P. CURRIE, THE CONSTITUTION IN THE SUPREME COURT: THE FIRST HUNDRED YEARS, 1789–1888 47–78 (1985).

17. 3 U.S. (3 Dall.) at 388.

18. CURRIE, *supra* note 16, at 46.

19. *See infra* at 28–32.

20. United States v. Heth, 3 Cranch 399, 413 (1806).

21. 6 Cranch 87, 135, 136 (1810).

22. 7 Johns. 477 (N.Y. 1811).

23. *Id.* at 505–06.

24. 13 U.S. (9 Cranch) 43 (1815).

25. *Id.* at 52 (emphasis added).

26. Inhabitants of Goshen v. Inhabitants of Stonington, 4 Conn. 209, 225, 10 Am. Dec. 121 (1822).

27. *Id.*

28. Argument in Wilkinson v. Leland, 2 Pet. 627 (1829).

29. *Id.* at 657. It must be recalled that, at the time, the Fifth Amendment's takings clause was only applied to actions by the federal government. Thus, neither Story nor Webster could rely on that provision as a basis for articulat-

ing limits on Rhode Island's power to adopt legislation. They therefore had to rely on more general notions of natural law.

30. *Id.*

31. *Id.* at 660.

32. JOSEPH STORY, COMMENTARIES ON THE CONSTITUTION 1, §§ 1398–99 (5th ed.), *quoted in Smith*, 5 TEX. L. REV. at 235.

33. Benson v. Mayor, etc. of New York, 10 Barb. 223 (N.Y. 1850).

34. POTTER'S DWARRIS ON STATUTES 162 (1885), *quoted in Smith*, 5 TEX. L. REV. at 235–36.

35. *Smith*, 5 TEX. L. REV. at 236.

36. Charles B. Hochman, *The Supreme Court and the Constitutionality of Retroactive Legislation,* 73 HARV. L. REV. 692, 694 (*citing* League v. Texas, 184 U.S. 156, 161 (1902)) [hereinafter *Hochman*] ("[A] Statute of a State is not brought into conflict with the Federal Constitution by the mere fact that it is retroactive. . . ."); Baltimore & S.R.R. v. Nesbit, 51 U.S. 395, 401 (1851) (only constitutional bars to retroactive state laws are ex post facto and contracts clauses).

37. 15 How. 421, 14 L.Ed. 755 (1854).

38. *Id.* at 423.

39. These are cited and discussed in Kaiser Aluminum v. Bonjorno, 494 U.S. 827, 842–45 (1990) (Scalia, J., concurring).

40. 191 U.S. 545, 552 (1903).

41. 209 U.S. 306, 314 (1908).

42. 231 U.S. 190, 199 (1913).

43. 258 U.S. 529, 534–35 (1922).

44. 294 U.S. 435 (1935).

45. *Hochman*, 73 HARV. L. REV. at 706.

46. United States v. Darusmont, 449 U.S. 292, 296 (1981).

47. *Id.*

48. *See, e.g.*, Nichols v. Coolidge, 274 U.S. 531 (1927); *see* Laura Ricciardi & Michael B. W. Sinclair, *Retroactive Civil Legislation,* 27 U. TOL. L. REV. 301, 350–57.

49. Cooper v. United States, 280 U.S. 409 (1930).

50. Milliken v. United States, 283 U.S. 15 (1931).

51. 283 U.S. 15 (1931).

52. Frederick A. Ballard, *Retroactive Federal Taxation,* 48 HARV. L. REV. 592 (1935).

53. 305 U.S. 134 (1938).

54. *Id.* at 146–47.

55. Tate & Lyle v. Commissioner of Internal Revenue, 87 F.3d 99, 106–07 (3rd Cir. 1996) (upholding application of a treasury regulation limiting the availability of certain interest deductions that was released in final form on January 5, 1993, which was retroactive to tax years beginning after December 31, 1983).

56. 305 U.S. at 144.

57. United States v. Darusmont, 449 U.S. at 297; United States v. Hudson, 299 U.S. 498 (1937) (recognizing that Congress has routinely made tax legis-

lation retroactive "for relatively short periods so as to include profits from transactions consummated while the statute was in process of enactment, or within so much of the calendar year as preceded the enactment").

58. WILLIAM LEUCHTENBERG, THE SUPREME COURT REBORN 220–28 (1995).

59. WILLIAM N. ESKRIDGE, JR. & PHILIP P. FRICKEY, CASES AND MATERIALS ON LEGISLATION: STATUTES AND THE CREATION OF PUBLIC POLICY 275 (1988).

60. *Bonjorno*, 494 U.S. at 844 (Scalia, J., concurring).

61. 379 U.S. 497 (1965).

62. In dissent, Justice Black condemned the Court for "through its balancing process stat[ing] the case in a way inevitably destined to bypass the Contract Clause and let Texas break its solemn obligation." He thought Texas had to compensate the landowners "for the contractual rights it wants to destroy."

63. 376 U.S. 149 (1964).

64. *Id.* (*quoting* Union Pacific R.R. Co. v. Laramie Stock Yards Co., 231 U.S. 190, 199 (1913)).

65. *See, e.g.*, Troy Ltd. v. Renna, 727 F.2d 287 (3d Cir. 1984) (upholding against a contract clause claim a tenancy act that retrospectively conferred on citizens over sixty years old special rights with respect to evictions upon condominium conversions).

66. *See, e.g.*, N.A. Burkitt, Inc. v. J. I. Case Co., 597 F. Supp. 1086 (D. Me. 1984) (upholding state law requiring that a dealer be given a six-month opportunity to cure performance before cancellation for poor performance); Energy Reserves v. Kansas Power and Light Co., 459 U.S. 400 (1983) (refusing to strike down legislation abrogating price redetermination clauses in a contract between a utility and a gas supplier).

67. East N.Y. Sav. Bank v. Hahn, 326 U.S. 230 (1945).

68. Faitoute Iron & Steel Co. v. City of Asbury Park, 316 U.S. 502 (1942).

69. *See, e.g.*, City of El Paso v. Simons, 379 U.S. 497, 508–09 (1965) (impairment of land purchaser's bargained-for right to reinstatement was held reasonable).

70. Nelson Lund, *Retroactivity, Institutional Incentives, and the Politics of Civil Rights*, 1995 PUB. INTEREST L. REV. 87, 88.

71. *Id.*

72. 393 U.S. 268 (1969).

73. *Id.* at 272.

74. 5 U.S. (1 Cranch) 103 (1801).

75. *Id.* at 281.

76. 416 U.S. 696 (1974).

77. *Id.* at 712–15.

78. *Bradley*, 416 U.S. at 716; *Thorpe*, 393 U.S. at 282.

79. *Bradley*, 416 U.S. at 717.

80. *Id.* at 849.

81. *See* Antonin Scalia, *The Rule of Law as a Law of Rules*, 56 U. CHI. L. REV. 1175 (1989); *Bonjorno*, 494 U.S. at 827 (Scalia, J., concurring) ("'Manifest injustice,' I fear, is just a surrogate for policy preferences. Indeed it cannot be otherwise.").

82. Bennett v. New Jersey, 470 U.S. 632 (1985). Llewellyn had contrasted

the presumption of prospectivity with the maxim that remedial statutes are to be applied retroactively.

83. *Luneberg*, 1991 DUKE L.J. at 125.

84. 428 U.S. 1 (1976).

85. United States v. Northeastern Pharm. and Chem. Co., 579 F. Supp. 823, 838 n.15 (W.D. Mo. 1984).

86. 42 U.S.C. § 9607 (1988 & Supp. V 1993).

87. Brown v. Georgeoff, 562 F. Supp. 1300 (N.D. Ohio 1983).

88. *Id.* at 1311.

89. *See, e.g.*, Brown v. Georgeoff, 562 F. Supp. at 1309–14. Although not the earliest case, *Georgeoff* contains the most extended discussion of section 107's legislative history and is one of the cases most often cited in subsequent decisions. *See, e.g.*, United States v. Northeastern Pharmaceutical, 810 F.2d 726, 732–33 (8th Cir. 1986); O'Neil v. Picillo, 682 F. Supp. 706, 729 (D.R.I. 1988); United States v. Ward, 618 F. Supp. 884, 898 (D.N.C. 1985); Kelley v. Thomas Solvent Co., 714 F. Supp. 1439, 1443 (W.D. Mich. 1989); Amy Blaymore, *Retroactive Application of Superfund: Can Old Dogs Be Taught New Tricks?*, B.C. ENVTL. AFF. L. REV. 1 (1985). *See also* United States v. South Carolina Recycling & Disposal, 20 Env't Rep. Cas. (BNA) 1753 (D.S.C. Feb. 23, 1984).

90. *See* Cathleen Clark, *Should the Butcher, the Baker, and the Candlestick Maker Be Held Responsible for Hazardous Waste?*, 1994 UTAH L. REV. 871 (1994).

91. *See* Mark Reisch & David M. Bearden, *CRS Report to Congress*, SUPERFUND FACT BOOK, ENR 97-312, Mar. 1997 at 17.

92. *See* GAO, Superfund Legal Expenses for Cleanup-Related Activities of Major U.S. Corporations, GAO-RCED-95-46, Dec. 1994, at 38.

93. *See, e.g.*, Jerry Taylor, *Symposium*, INSIGHT MAG., May 1, 1995 ("Superfund has bankrupted hundreds of small companies and threatens thousands more. . . ."); *Recent Developments in the News*, 23 ENVTL. L. REP. 10519 (August 1993) (reporting Superfund settlement with bankrupt company Insilco Corp.); Peter Fairley, *Small Business Is Beautiful in Washington*, CHEM. WK., April 30, 1997, at 056 (reporting "bipartisan support on Capitol Hill to write small companies out of Superfund's liability web altogether").

94. U.S. GENERAL ACCOUNTING OFFICE, HAZARDOUS WASTE, ENVIRONMENTAL SAFEGUARDS JEOPARDIZED WHEN FACILITIES CEASE OPERATING 18 (1986).

95. *Id.*; *see also CERCLA Liability May Arise from Sale of Used Batteries*, BNA BANKING REP., Aug. 29, 1994, at 296 (discussing lenders' reactions to CERCLA).

96. EPA, Superfund Response Action Contractor Indemnification, 54 Fed. Reg. 46,012, 46,013 (Oct. 31, 1989).

97. 488 U.S. 204 (1988).

98. 488 U.S. at 208. Some of the hope that *Bowen* inspired needs to be tempered, at least in the administrative context, by the Supreme Court's recent decision in Smiley v. Citibank (South Dakota), N.A., 116 S. Ct. 1730 (1996). The question in *Smiley* was whether a statute permitting banks to charge out-of-state customers the amount of "interest" on credit cards that

they could charge in-state customers covered late fees as well. At the time the late fee was charged to an out-of-state customer, there was no agency guidance on the subject. Nonetheless, the Court deferred to the agency's regulation interpreting the term *interest* as including late fees, even though that regulation had been adopted after the relevant event—the charging of the fee —had taken place. The Court rejected the argument that deferring to a regulation involving past transactions would make the regulation retroactive in violation of *Bowen*. 116 S. Ct. at 1735 n.3 (noting, however, that "[t]here might be substance to this point if the regulation replaced a prior agency interpretation—which, as we have discussed, it did not").

99. *Bonjorno*, 494 U.S. at 842.

100. *Id.* at 838 (citations omitted).

101. 511 U.S. 244 (1994).

102. *Id.* at 256, 260 ("It is entirely possible—indeed, highly probable— that, because it was unable to resolve the retroactivity issue with the clarity of the 1990 legislation, Congress viewed the matter as an open issue to be resolved by the courts.")

103. *Id.* at 261.

104. *Id.* at 280 (emphasis added).

105. *Id.* at 283–84.

106. *Id.* at 275.

107. *Id.* at 287 (Scalia, J., concurring).

108. *Id.*

109. *Id.* at 289.

110. United States v. $814,254.76 in U.S. Currency (Banamex), 51 F.3d 207 (9th Cir. 1995).

111. James Cable Partners v. City of Jamestown, 43 F.3d 277, 279 (6th Cir. 1995).

112. 117 S. Ct. 1871 (1997).

113. *Id.* at *5.

114. *Landgraf*, 511 U.S. at 280.

115. *Lund*, 1995 PUB. INTEREST L. REV. at 95.

116. *Id.*

117. *Landgraf*, 511 U.S. at 244.

CHAPTER 4: EX POST FACTO CLAUSES

1. *See supra* at 27–28.

2. WILLIAM W. CROSSKEY, POLITICS AND THE CONSTITUTION IN THE HISTORY OF THE UNITED STATES 325 (1953).

3. *Records of the Federal Constitution* 2:375; Madison, 22 Aug., *in* PHILIP B. KURLAND & RALPH LERNER, 3 THE FOUNDERS' CONSTITUTION 347 (1987) [hereinafter KURLAND & LERNER].

4. *Id.*

5. *Id.*

6. *Id.*

7. *Id.*

8. *Id.*

9. *Id.*

10. *Id.*

11. *Id.* 2:448 Madison, 29 Aug.

12. *See infra* at 51.

13. *Records of the Federal Convention* 2:617 Madison, 14 Sept., *in* KURLAND & LERNER at 347.

14. *Id.* 2:640 Mason, 15 Sept.

15. For a penetrating analysis of this case, on which my discussion heavily relies, *see* DAVID P. CURRIE, THE CONSTITUTION IN THE SUPREME COURT: THE FIRST HUNDRED YEARS, 1789–1888 42–43 (1986).

16. 3 U.S. (3 Dall.) at 391.

17. *Id.* at 391–92.

18. 3 U.S. (3 Dall.) at 396–97.

19. *Id.* at 399–400.

20. 27 U.S. (2 Pet.) 380 at 916 a (1829) (separate statement of William Johnson).

21. *See, e.g.,* Fletcher v. Peck, 10 U.S. (Cranch) 87, 131 ("An ex post facto law is one which renders an act punishable in a manner in which it was not punishable when committed. Such a law may inflict penalties on the person, or may inflict pecuniary penalties which swell the public treasury.").

22. Carpenter v. Pennsylvania, 58 U.S. (17 How.) 456, 463 (1854).

23. *Id.* (citations omitted).

24. *See, e.g.,* Laura Ricciardi & Michael B. W. Sinclair, *Retroactive Civil Legislation*, 27 U. TOL. L. REV. 301 (1996) [hereinafter *Ricciardi & Sinclair*] (reviewing the discussions about the ex post facto clause during the Convention and ratification debates and concluding that it applied to civil laws as well; also taking issue with the contention that *Calder* disposed of the question).

25. 27 U.S. (2 Pet.) 380 (1829).

26. *Id.* at 915.

27. *Id.*

28. *Id.* at 916 b.

29. *Id.*

30. *Id.* at 915 c.

31. *Id.*

32. *Id.*

33. *Id.*

34. *Ricciardi & Sinclair*, 27 U. TOL. L. REV. at 316–18.

35. *Id.* at 318.

36. To some extent, Justices Black and Douglas also thought that the ex post facto clauses apply to civil legislation. *See, e.g.,* Lehmann v. Carlson, 353 U.S. 685, 690–91 (1957) (Black, J., concurring) (urging the Court to reconsider its interpretation with a view to applying it to protect individuals more effectively from new or additional burdens retrospectively imposed by Congress); Marecello v. Bonds, 349 U.S. 302, 319 (1955) (Douglas, J., dissenting) (urging broader application of the clause to fulfill its original intention).

37. W. W. CROSSKEY, POLITICS AND THE CONSTITUTION IN THE HISTORY OF THE UNITED STATES at 335 (*quoting* George Mason).

38. *Id.* at 352–60.

39. 3 U.S. (3 Dall.) at 391.

40. *See generally* Paul Brest, *The Misconceived Quest for the Original Understanding*, 60 B.U. L. REV. 204 (1980).

41. Oliver P. Field, *Ex Post Facto in the Constitution*, 20 MICH. L. REV. 315, 321 (1921).

42. *See, e.g.*, Harisiades v. Shaughnessy, 342 U.S. 580, 595 (1952).

43. Weaver v. Graham, 450 U.S. 24, 31 (1980).

44. *See, e.g.*, Louis Vuitton v. Spencer Handbags Corp., 765 F.2d 966 (2d Cir. 1985) (construing as prospective a statute increasing the penalty for counterfeiting to treble damages to avoid the ex post facto and due process issues that would have been created by retrospective application of the statute).

45. Flemming v. Nestor, 363 U.S. 603, 613–14 (1960).

46. DeVeau v. Braisted, 363 U.S. 144, 160 (1960) (plurality opinion of Frankfurter, J.) (holding that a bar on felons holding office in a waterfront labor organization was neither an ex post facto law nor a bill of attainder).

47. U.S. Const. amend. V.

48. *See* United States v. Ursery, 116 S. Ct. 2135 (1996) (Scalia, J., concurring).

49. *Id.*

50. *See, e.g.*, Bae v. Shalala, 44 F.3d 489, 492–93 (7th Cir. 1995).

51. 490 U.S. 435, 447–48 (1989).

52. *Id.*, at 447–49 (citations and footnotes omitted).

53. *Ursery*, 116 S. Ct. 2135 (1996).

54. *Id.*

55. *Id.*

56. *Halper*, 490 U.S. at 449 (emphasis added).

57. The ex post facto clause is neither discussed nor cited in *Ursery*, 116 S. Ct. 2135 (1996).

58. *Ricciardi & Sinclair*, 27 U. TOL. L. REV. at 325.

CHAPTER 5: BILL OF ATTAINDER CLAUSES

1. "No Bill of Attainder . . . shall be passed." U.S. Const. art. I, § 9, cl. 3.

2. Raoul Berger, *Bills of Attainder: A Study of Amendment by the Court*, 63 CORNELL L. REV. 355, 373–76 (1978) [hereinafter *Berger*].

3. 1 Jac. 2, c. 2 (1685), *quoted in* Nixon v. Administrator of General Services, 433 U.S. 425, 475 (1977).

4. *Berger*, 63 CORNELL L. REV. at 373–76.

5. *Id.* at 37.

6. *Id.* at 379.

7. Fletcher v. Peck, 10 U.S. 87, 137 (1810).

8. Cummings v. Missouri, 71 U.S. 277, 323 (1866).

9. *Id.*

10. *Id.* at 332.

11. *Ex parte* Garland, 71 U.S. 333, 381 (1866).

12. *Id.* at 377; *Cummings*, 71 U.S. at 325.

13. United States v. Brown, 381 U.S. 437, 442 (1965).

14. *Id.* at 446.

15. *Id.* at 461–62.

16. *Id.* at 455–56.

17. Nixon v. Administrator of General Services, 433 U.S. 425, 468 (1977).

18. Selective Service System v. Minnesota Public Interest Research Group, 468 U.S. 841, 846 (1984).

19. *See supra* at 53–55.

20. *Id.* at 852.

21. *Nixon*, 433 U.S. at 483.

CHAPTER 6: CONTRACTS CLAUSE

1. U.S. Const. art. I, §9. There are at least four excellent articles on the contracts clause. They are Douglas W. Kmiec & John O. McGinnis, *The Contract Clause: A Return to Original Understanding*, 14 HASTINGS CONST. L.Q. 525 (1987) [hereinafter *Kmiec & McGinnis*]; Michael McConnell, *Contract Rights and Property Rights: A Case Study in the Relationship Between Individual Liberties and Constitutional Structure*, 76 CALIF. L. REV. 267, 286 (1988); Richard Epstein, *Toward a Revitalization of the Contract Clause*, 51 U. CHI. L. REV. 703 (1994) [hereinafter *Epstein*]; Michael B. Rappaport, *A Procedural Approach to the Contract Clause*, 93 YALE L.J. 918 (1984) [hereinafter *Rappaport*].

2. THE FEDERALIST PAPERS, No. 10, at 83 (Madison).

3. *Compare Epstein*, 51 U. CHI. L. REV., at 723–25 (arguing for the Clause's prospective application) *with Kmiec & McGinnis*, 14 HASTINGS CONST. L.Q. at 557–59 (responding to Professor Epstein).

4. *Kmiec & McGinnis*, 14 HASTINGS CONST. L.Q. at 526.

5. *Id.*

6. *See, e.g., Epstein*, 51 U. CHI. L. REV. at 706.

7. An Ordinance for the Government of the Territory of the United States North-West of the River Ohio, 1 Stat. 51 (1787).

8. *Records of the Federal Convention*, 2:439; Madison, 28 Aug., *in* PHILIP B. KURLAND & RALPH LERNER, THE FOUNDERS' CONSTITUTION 393 (1987).

9. *Id.*

10. *Id.*

11. *Id.*

12. *Id.* 2:448; Madison, 29 Aug.; *see supra* at 49.

13. *Id.* 2:619, Madison, 14 Sept.

14. *Id.*

15. *Kmiec & McGinnis*, 14 HASTINGS CONST. L.Q. at 535; *see also* DAVID P. CURRIE, THE CONSTITUTION IN THE SUPREME COURT: THE FIRST 100 YEARS, 1789–1888 128 (1986).

16. 10 U.S. (6 Cranch) 87 (1810).

17. *Id.*

18. 17 U.S. (4 Wheat) 122 (1819).

19. 17 U.S. (4 Wheat) 518 (1819).

20. *Kmiec & McGinnis*, 14 HASTINGS CONST. L.Q. at 538–40.

21. The details of the individual cases, and specific quarrels with aspects of the Marshall Court's contracts clause interpretation, are not important here.

22. *Id.* at 538.

23. *See, e.g.*, JAMES MCPHERSON, BATTLE CRY OF FREEDOM 859 (1988); Mugler v. Kansas, 123 U.S. 623 (1887).

24. 101 U.S. 814 (1879).

25. *Kmiec & McGinnis*, 14 HASTINGS CONST. L.Q. at 540–41.

26. *See, e.g.*, Smyth v. Ames, 169 U.S. 466, 526 (1897) (using economic substantive due process to analyze the regulation of railroad rates).

27. *Rappaport*, 93 YALE L.J. 918, 924 (1984) (citing cases); Allied Structural Steel v. Spannaus, 438 U.S. 234, 241 (1978) ("[T]he Contract Clause receded into comparative desuetude with the development of the large body of jurisprudence under the Due Process Clause . . . in modern constitutional history.").

28. *Kmiec & McGinnis*, 14 HASTINGS CONST. L.Q. at 526.

29. 290 U.S. 398 (1934).

30. *Blaisdell*, 290 U.S. at 443 (*quoting* Missouri v. Holland, 252 U.S. 416, 433 (1920)).

31. *Id.* at 447.

32. 292 U.S. 426 (1934).

33. W. B. Worthen Co. v. Kavanaugh, 295 U.S. 56 (1935).

34. Triegle v. Acme Homestead Ass'n, 297 U.S. 189 (1936).

35. *See supra* at 35–36.

36. W. David Slawson, *Constitutional and Legislative Considerations in Retroactive Lawmaking*, 48 CALIF. L. REV. 216, 221.

37. 431 U.S. 1 (1977).

38. 431 U.S. at 25.

39. 431 U.S. at 30–32.

40. Allied Structural Steel v. Spannaus, 438 U.S. 234 (1978).

41. *Kmiec & McGinnis*, 14 HASTINGS CONST. L.Q. at 545; *see also Rappaport*, 93 YALE L.J. at 920 ("[E]xcessive discretion generates uncertainty, undermines the goals of a written Constitution, and impairs the rule of law.").

42. Green v. Biddle, 21 U.S. (8 Wheat) 1, 84 (1823) (Washington, J.) (defining an "impairment of the obligation" of contract).

CHAPTER 7: UNCOMPENSATED TAKINGS

1. Daniel Webster, *Argument in Wilkinson v. Leland*, 2 Pet. 627 (1829).

2. *See generally* Michael W. McConnell, *Contract Rights and Property Rights: A Case Study in the Relationship Between Individual Liberties and Constitutional Structure*, 76 CALIF. L. REV. 267 (1988).

3. Chicago, Burlington and Quincy R.R. Co. v. Chicago, 166 U.S. 226, 241 (1897).

4. *Quoted in* MARK L. POLLOT, GRAND THEFT & PETITE LARCENY: PROPERTY RIGHTS IN AMERICA (1993) 34–35.

5. 28 Edw. III, ch. 3 (1335).

6. RICHARD EPSTEIN, TAKINGS: PRIVATE PROPERTY AND THE POWER OF EMINENT DOMAIN 10 (1985) [hereinafter EPSTEIN, TAKINGS].

7. JOHN LOCKE, SECOND TREATISE OF GOVERNMENT, ch. 5 (1980).

8. *Id.,* § 27.

9. EPSTEIN, TAKINGS, at 16.

10. *Id.*

11. WILLIAM PENN, ENGLAND'S PRESENT INTEREST CONSIDERED (1675).

12. JAMES MADISON, NOTES OF DEBATES IN THE FEDERAL CONVENTION 244 (1987).

13. 4 THE JAMES MADISON LETTERS 478 (1792), *quoted* in POLLOT, *supra* note 4, at 37.

14. JAMES MADISON, *supra* note 12, at 312.

15. Barron v. Mayor of Baltimore, 32 U.S. 243 (1833).

16. West River Bridge v. Dix, 6 How. 507 (U.S. 1848).

17. James v. Campbell, 104 U.S. 356, 358 (1881) ("The government of the United States, as well as the citizen, is subject to the Constitution; and when it grants a patent the grantee is entitled to it as a matter of right, and does not receive it, as was originally supposed to be the case in England, as a matter of grace and favor."); Solomons v. United States, 137 U.S. 342, 346 (1890) ("The government has no more power to appropriate a man's property invested in a patent than it has to take his property invested in real estate. . . .").

18. Harry N. Scheiber, *The "Takings" Clause and the Fifth Amendment: Original Intent and Significance in American Legal Development, in* THE BILL OF RIGHTS: ORIGINAL MEANING AND CURRENT UNDERSTANDING 233, 240 (Eugene W. Hicock, Jr., ed., 1991) [hereinafter *Takings Clause*]; *see also* Harry N. Scheiber, *The Road to Munn: Eminent Domain and the Concept of Public Purpose in the State Courts,* 5 PERSPECTIVES IN AMERICAN HISTORY 327–402 (1971); William Michael Treanor, *The Origins and Original Significance of the Just Compensation Clause of the Fifth Amendment,* 94 YALE L.J. 694 (1985).

19. Scheiber, *Takings Clause* at 242.

20. *See* Lucas v. South Carolina Coastal Council, 505 U.S. 1003, 1014 (1992) (*citing* Legal Tender Cases, 12 Wall. 457, 551 (1871) and Transportation Co. v. Chicago, 99 U.S. 635, 642 (1879)).

21. 123 U.S. 623, 668–69 (1887).

22. 260 U.S. 393 (1922).

23. J. Gregory Sidak & Daniel F. Spulber, *Deregulatory Takings and Breach of the Regulatory Contract,* 71 N.Y.U. L. REV. at 856 [hereinafter *Sidak & Spulber*].

24. *Id.*

25. 260 U.S. at 414.

26. *Id.*

27. *Lucas,* 505 U.S. at 1015 (quotation marks, brackets, ellipses, and citations omitted).

28. 438 U.S. 104 (1978).

29. *Id.* at 124–25 (citation omitted).

30. *See, e.g., Sidak & Spulber*, 71 N.Y.U. L. REV.; EPSTEIN, TAKINGS.

31. *Lucas*, 505 U.S. at 1014.

32. *See, e.g.*, Loretto v. Teleprompter Manhattan CATV Corp., 458 U.S. 419 (1982) (law requiring landlords to allow television cable companies to place cable facilities in their apartment building constituted a taking).

33. *Lucas*, 505 U.S. at 1014.

34. 116 S. Ct. 2432 (1996).

35. PUB. L. 101-73, 103 Stat. 183 (1989).

CHAPTER 8: SEPARATION OF POWERS

1. *But see* Justice Chase in Calder v. Bull, 3 U.S. 386, 388 (1798) ("for I cannot call it a law").

2. *See supra* at 28–32; and *infra* at 76–80.

3. U.S. Const. art. III.

4. 13 Wall. 128 (1872). *See also Hayburn's Case*, 2 Dall. 409 (1792) (Congress may not vest review of the decisions of Article III judges in executive branch officials).

5. *Klein*, 13 Wall. at 146.

6. Robertson v. Seattle Audubon Society, 503 U.S. 429, 441 (1992).

7. 514 U.S. 211 (1995).

8. *Id.* at 225.

9. *Id.* That discussion will not be repeated here.

10. *Id.*, at 224.

11. *Id.* (*quoting* THE FEDERALIST, No. 81).

12. John Hart Ely, DEMOCRACY AND DISTRUST 18 (1980).

13. BLACKSTONE, COMMENTARIES 1:137–38.

14. Delaware Declaration of Rights and Fundamental Rules, 11 Sept. 1797, *in* PHILIP B. KURLAND & RALPH LERNER, 3 THE FOUNDERS' CONSTITUTION 312 (1987) (hereinafter KURLAND & LERNER).

15. Alexander Hamilton, *Remarks on an Act for Regulating Elections*, New York Assembly, 6 Feb. 1787, *in* KURLAND & LERNER at 313.

16. *See supra* at 28–32.

17. 123 U.S. 623 (1887); *see supra* at 69–70.

18. I am indebted to Professor John Harrison for this analysis.

19. Planned Parenthood v. Casey, 505 U.S. 833 (1992) (citation omitted) ("Although a literal reading of the [Due Process] Clause might suggest that it governs only the procedures by which a State may deprive persons of liberty, for at least 105 years, at least since Mugler v. Kansas, 123 U.S. 623 [in 1887], the Clause has been understood to contain a substantive component as well. . . .").

20. Ray H. Greenblatt, *Judicial Limitations on Retroactive Civil Legislation*, 51 Nw. U. L. REV. 540, 543 (1956).

21. Noble v. Union River Logging R.R., 147 U.S. 165 (1893).

22. Lynch v. United States, 292 U.S. 571, 579 (1934); Perry v. United States, 294 U.S. 330 (1935).

23. 305 U.S. 134 (1938).

24. Andrew Weiler, *Has Due Process Struck Out? The Judicial Rubber-*

stamping of Retroactive Economic Laws, 42 DUKE L.J. 1069, 1071–72 (1993) (footnotes omitted).

25. *Smith*, 5 TEX. L. REV. at 231.

26. BLACK'S LAW DICTIONARY 1564 (6th ed. 1990).

27. SINGER, SUTHERLAND STAT. CONST. ¶ 41.06 (5th ed. 1992).

28. *Id.*

29. Usery v. Turner Elkhorn Mining Co., 428 U.S. 1, 16–17 (1976).

30. Eule, *Temporal Limits on the Legislative Mandate: Entrenchment and Retroactivity*, 1987 AMER. BAR FOUND. RES. J. at 429 [hereinafter *Eule*].

31. 512 U.S. 26, 32 (1994). For a devastating critique of the Supreme Court's decision in *Carlton, see* Laura Ricciardi & Michael B. W. Sinclair, *Retroactive Civil Legislation,* 27 U. TOL. L. REV. 301 (1996) at 357–74.

32. United States v. Carlton, 512 U.S. 26, 40 (1994) (Scalia, J., concurring).

33. *Bowen*, 488 U.S. 204, 224 (Scalia, J.) (*citing* Pension Benefit Guaranty Corp., 467 U.S. 717 (1982) and Usery v. Turner Elkhorn Mining Co., 428 U.S. 1 (1976)).

34. *See* Pension Benefit Guaranty Corp. v. R.A. Gray & Co., 467 U.S. 717, 729–30 (1982); *Eule*, 1987 AM. BAR. FOUND. RES. J. at 429 ("Minimal scrutiny is still very much the order of the day.").

35. A. B. Small Co. v. American Sugar Refining Co., 267 U.S. 233, 239 (1925) (*quoting* United States v. Cohen Grocery Co., 255 U.S. 81, 89 (1921)).

36. 267 U.S. 233, 239 (1925).

37. *Id.* at 239.

38. Gates & Fox Co. v. OSHRC, 790 F.2d 154, 156 (D.C. Cir. 1986).

39. 937 F.2d 649 (D.C. Cir. 1991).

40. *Id.* at 651, *quoting* 40 C.F.R. § 761.79(a) (emphasis added by the court).

41. *Id.* at 651.

42. *Id.* (quotation marks omitted).

43. *Id.* at 652.

44. For a compelling argument that current law should be changed and that agencies should not be accorded deference in the interpretation of their own regulations, see John F. Manning, *Constitutional Structure and Judicial Deference to Agency Interpretations of Agency Rules*, 96 COLUM. L. REV. 612.

45. *Rollins*, 937 F.2d at 651–52 (quotation marks omitted).

46. *Id.* at 653.

47. *Id.* at 655 (Edwards, J., concurring in part and dissenting in part).

48. *Id.* at 655.

49. General Electric v. EPA, 53 F.3d 1324 (D.C. Cir. 1995).

50. *Id.* at 1329 (quotations omitted and citing, *inter alia*, Radio Athens Inc. v. FCC, 401 F.2d 398 (D.C. Cir. 1968), where the court set aside the dismissal of a petitioner's application for a radio license).

CHAPTER 9: CASE OF SUPERFUND

1. *See supra* at 6, 38–39.

2. George Clemon Freeman, Jr., *Inappropriate and Unconstitutional Retroactive Application of Superfund Liability*, 42 BUS. LAW. 215 (Nov. 1986) [here-

inafter *Freeman, Liability*]; George Clemon Freeman, Jr., *A Public Policy Essay: Superfund Retroactivity Revisited*, 50 Bus. Law. 663 (Feb. 1995) [hereinafter *Freeman, Retroactivity*].

3. United States v. Olin Corp., 927 F. Supp. 1502 (S.D. Ala. 1996). After this manuscript had been commissioned, my firm was asked to submit an *amicus curiae* brief in this case on behalf of a long-standing client, the Insurance Environmental Litigation Association. I played a role in drafting that brief, which contends that CERCLA should not be applied retroactively.

4. *Freeman, Liability*, 42 Bus. Law. at 221–22.

5. *Landgraf*, 511 U.S. at 257; *see supra* at 40–42.

6. *Freeman, Liability*, 42 Bus. Law at 223.

7. *Id*. This discussion is expanded upon in Freeman, *Retroactivity*, 50 Bus. Law. at 672–78.

8. United States v. Northeastern Pharm. & Chem. Co., 579 F. Supp. 823, 839–41 (W.D. Mo. 1984).

9. *Freeman, Liability*, 42 Bus. Law at 216.

10. 26 U.S.C. § 59A (1988) (establishing an environmental tax on corporations equal to 0.12% of taxable income over $2 million; 26 U.S.C. §§ 4611(a), 4611(c)(2) (imposing 9.7 cents per barrel tax on petroleum products); 26 U.S.C. §§ 4661, 4671 (establishing a tax on all chemicals sold by or used by a manufacturer or importer of chemicals); 26 U.S.C. § 9507(b)(1) (transferring to the Superfund the money raised by the above taxes); *see generally* David H. Topol, *Hazardous Waste and Bankruptcy: Confronting the Unasked Questions*, 13 Va. Envtl. L.J. 185, 189 (1994).

11. *See, e.g.*, Brown Eng'g v. Estate of Reeve, 799 F. Supp. 467 (D.N.J. 1992); Kelley v. Thomas Solvent Co., 619 F. Supp. 162, 220 (W.D. Mo. 1985); Northeastern Pharm. & Chem. Co., 579 F. Supp. 823, 839 (W.D. Mo. 1984); State ex rel. Brown v. Georgeoff, 562 F. Supp. 1300 (N.D. Ohio 1983).

12. *See, e.g.*, United States v. South Carolina Recycling & Disposal, Inc., 653 F. Supp. 984 (D.S.C. 1984), *aff'd in part sub nom.*, United States v. Monsanto, 858 F.2d 160 (4th Cir. 1988), *cert. denied*, 490 U.S. 1106 (1989); United States v. Price, 523 F. Supp. 1055 (D.N.J. 1981), *aff'd*, 688 F.2d 204 (3d Cir. 1982).

13. United States v. Olin Corp., 927 F. Supp. 1502 (S.D. Ala. 1996).

14. *Olin*, 927 F. Supp. at 1504. The government contended that 1,500 acres in McIntosh, Alabama, were contaminated by the operations of a mercury-cell chloralkali plant, which was active from 1952 to 1974, and from a second plant that operated there from 1955 to 1982.

15. *Id*. at 1518–19 (*quoting Landgraf*, 511 U.S. at 286).

16. 114 S. Ct. 1483 (1994).

17. *Olin*, 927 F. Supp. at 1519.

18. *Freeman, Retroactivity*, 50 Bus. Law 664 (1995).

19. United States v. Olin, 107 F.3d 1506, 1512 (11th Cir. 1997).

20. *Id*. at 153.

21. George Freeman's article attacking the constitutionality of CERCLA, which was adapted from his brief on the subject, makes a variety of other arguments against applying CERCLA retroactively that are not relevant here, such as the contention that CERCLA is a "standardless delegation" in viola-

tion of the separation of powers or that CERCLA may violate the prohibition on "excessive fines." *Freeman, Liability*, 42 Bus. Law. at 229, 239.

22. *Id.* at 237.

23. *See* David H. Topol, *Hazardous Waste and Bankruptcy: Confronting the Unasked Questions*, 13 Va. Envtl. L.J. 185 (1994); Viki Reath, *Could Affect Superfund Reform SEC May Force Firms to List Environmental Liabilities*, Env't Wk., Apr. 6, 1995; Associated Press, *Cleanup Financing Settled/Superfund Site Bill to Top $6 Million*, Telegram & Gazette (Worcester), Oct. 29, 1994, at A13; Ted Cilwick, *Superfund Nightmare Utah's Ekotek Mess a Perfect Example: Gunky Ground, Filthy Financing*, Salt Lake Trib., Nov. 8, 1992, at A1; *see also In re* Chateaugay Corp., 944 F.2d 997 (2d Cir. 1991); Ninth Ave. Remedial Group v. Allis-Chalmers Corp., 195 B.R. 716 (N.D. Ind. 1996); *In re* National Gypsum Co. 139 B.R. 397 (N.D. Tex. 1992).

24. *See* Mark Reisch & David M. Bearden, *CRS Report to Congress*, Superfund Fact Book, ENR 97-312, Mar. 1997, at 17.

25. Jerry Taylor, *Is It Time to Repeal Superfund and Give Cleanup Costs to the States? Yes. State Cleanups Are Cheaper and Faster*, Insight Mag., May 1, 1995, at 18.

26. *See* GAO, *Superfund: Legal Expenses for Cleanup-Related Activities of Major U.S. Corporations*, GAO/RCED-95-46, Dec. 1994, at 38.

27. *See* Peter Fairley, *Small Business Is Beautiful in Washington*, 159, Chem. Wk. 056 (Apr. 30, 1997); Abel Banov, *Powerful Voice Joins Superfund-Reform Clamor*, 78, Am. Paint & Coatings J. 8 (Jan. 17, 1994); Taylor, *supra* note 25, at 18; Bob Anderson, *Bill Changes Liability on Superfund Cleanups*, Advoc. (Baton Rouge, La.), Oct. 1, 1995, at 1A.

28. United States v. Monsanto, 858 F.2d 160, 174 (4th Cir. 1988) ("Congress did not impose th[e] obligation [of restitution of cleanup costs] automatically on a legislatively defined class of persons.").

29. *Id.* at 446.

30. *See supra* at 56–58.

31. *Halper*, 490 U.S. at 449 (emphasis added). *See, e.g.*, United States v. Monsanto, 858 F.2d 160, 174 (4th Cir. 1988) ("The restitution of cleanup costs was not intended to operate, nor does it operate in fact, as a criminal penalty or a punitive deterrent.").

32. *Id.* at 238.

33. *See supra* at 77.

34. *See, e.g.*, Webb's Fabulous Pharmacies, Inc. v. Beckwith, 449 U.S. 155 (1980) (treating interest as property).

Chapter 10: A Suggestion for the Judiciary

1. Nelson Lund, *Retroactivity, Institutional Incentives, and the Politics of Civil Rights*, 1995 Pub. Interest L. Rev. 87, 95.

2. *Id.*

3. *See, e.g.*, United States v. Security Industrial Bank, 459 U.S. 70 (1982) (construing a statute prospectively to avoid having the statute raise a takings issue).

4. Note, *Intent, Clear Statement Rules, and the Common Law: Interpreta-*

tion in the Supreme Court, 95 HARV. L. REV. 892, 902 (1982) (*quoting Amtrak*, 414 U.S. at 458).

5. J. Gregory Sidak & Daniel F. Spulber, *Deregulatory Takings and Breach of the Regulatory Contract,* 71 N.Y.U. L. REV. 851, 940 (1996) [hereinafter *Sidak & Spulber*] (When "the losses associated with policy changes . . . are not compensated, policy changes (which is to say, regulation) is overconsumed relative to the level of regulation that would be demanded under a constitutional standard that required actual compensation for Pareto-efficient policy decisions.").

6. Loveladies Harbor, Inc. v. United States, 28 F.3d 1171 (Fed. Cir. 1994) (Plager, J.).

7. *Sidak & Spulber*, 71 N.Y.U. L. REV. at 944.

8. For a compelling argument that legislative supermajority provisions are constitutional, *see* John O. McGinnis & Michael B. Rappaport, *The Constitutionality of Legislative Supermajority Requirements: A Defense*, 105 YALE L.J. 483 (1995).

9. *Ricciardi & Sinclair*, 27 U. TOL. L. REV. at 341.

10. *Id.*

11. *Id.*

12. *See, e.g.,* 141 CONG. REC. S9981, 9982 (daily ed. July 14, 1995) (proposed amendment to S. 343 by Sen. Hutchinson); H.R. 2586, 104th Cong. Title II § 2005 (1995).

13. Kan. Stat. Ann. § 59-29a01 (1994).

14. The constitutionality of the law was upheld in Kansas v. Hendricks, 117 S. Ct. 2072 (1997).

15. The Supreme Court held that Kansas's statute did not violate the ex post facto law because it was a civil statute that was not punitive.

16. Kansas v. Hendrick, 117 S. Ct. 2072 (1997) (Breyer, J., joined by JJ. Stevens, Souter, and Ginsburg).

17. *See, e.g.,* 18 U.S.C. § 922(g)(9) (preventing anyone who had been convicted of domestic violence in the past from possessing a gun).

CHAPTER 11: CONCLUSION

1. Ray H. Greenblatt, *Judicial Limitations on Retroactive Civil Legislation*, 51 NW. U. L. REV. 540, 567 (1956).

INDEX

Thomas, Clarence, 54
Thorpe v. Housing Authority of Durham (1969), 36–40, 74
Toxic Substance Control Act (TSCA), 81
Tradition, Anglo-American, 1
Trumbull, H. Clay, 1
TSCA. *See* Toxic Substance Control Act

Union Pacific R. Co. v. Laramie Stock Yards Co. (1913), 33
United States Fidelity & Guaranty Co. v. United States ex rel. Struthers Wells Co. (1908), 32
United States Trust v. New Jersey (1977), 64
United States v. Carlton (1994), 79
United States v. Halper (1989), 54
United States v. Klein (1872), 73–74

United States v. Olin Corp. (1996), 83, 86–87
United States v. Winstar Corp. (1996), 71–72
Usery v. Turner Elkhorn Mining Co. (1976), 38

Warren Court. *See* Supreme Court
Warren, Earl, 12
W.B. Worthen Co. v. Thomas (1934), 64
Webster, Daniel, 30, 104n29
Welch v. Henry (1938), 34, 77
West River v. Dix (1848), 69
White v. United States (1903), 32
Wilkinson v. Leland (1829), 30–31
Wilkinson v. Meyer (1829), 51
Williamson, Hugh, 48
Wilson, James, 48, 61

ABOUT THE AUTHOR

Daniel E. Troy is an associate scholar of legal studies at the American Enterprise Institute and is a partner with Wiley, Rein & Fielding, where he specializes in constitutional and appellate litigation. From 1987 to 1989, Mr. Troy served as an attorney-adviser in the Department of Justice's Office of Legal Counsel. Mr. Troy was also special assistant to the 1989 Giuliani mayoral campaign and a member of the Committee on Reform of the Czechoslovakian Constitution. He is a former lecturer-in-law at his alma mater, the Columbia Law School. Mr. Troy clerked for Judge Robert H. Bork on the D.C. Circuit from 1983 to 1984.

A NOTE ON THE BOOK

This book was edited by
Cheryl Weissman of the publications staff
of the American Enterprise Institute.
The index was prepared by Julia Petrakis.
The text was set in Classic Garamond.
Electronic Quill set the type,
and Edwards Brothers, Incorporated,
printed and bound the book,
using permanent acid-free paper.

The AEI Press is the publisher for the American Enterprise Institute for Public Policy Research, 1150 Seventeenth Street, N.W., Washington, D.C. 20036; *Christopher DeMuth,* publisher; *Dana Lane,* director; *Ann Petty,* editor; *Leigh Tripoli,* editor; *Cheryl Weissman,* editor; *Alice Anne English,* production manager.

www.ingramcontent.com/pod-product-compliance
Lightning Source LLC
Jackson TN
JSHW011939131224
75386JS00041B/1463